Public Service Employment

The Experience of a Decade

Robert F. Cook
Charles F. Adams, Jr.
V. Lane Rawlins
and Associates

D1171545

W. E. Upjohn Institute for Employment Research

Library of Congress Cataloging in Publication Data

Cook, Robert F., 1945-
 Public service employment.

 1. Public service employment—United States.
 2. Manpower policy—united States. 4. United States—
 Full employment policies. 4. Occupational training—
 United States. I. Adams, Charles F., 1945-
 II. Rawlins, V. Lane. III. Title.
 HD5713.6.U54066 1985   331.13'77'0973   85-22495
 ISBN 0-88099-030-9
 ISBN 0-88099-031-7 (pbk.)

The Authors

Robert F. Cook is currently a senior economist with Westat, Inc. From 1976 through 1979 he was a research associate at the Brookings Institution and from 1979 through 1981 was a research economist in the Woodrow Wilson School of Public and International Affairs at Princeton University. He holds a Bachelors degree from the University of Maryland and a Doctorate in Business and Industrial Economics from Lehigh University.

Charles F. Adams, Jr., is associate professor in the School of Public Administration at The Ohio State University. He was formerly a research fellow at the Brookings Institution. His research interests focus on state and local public finance, with emphasis on intergovernmental fiscal relations. Professor Adams is co-author of *Revenue Sharing: The Second Round* (Brookings 1977).

V. Lane Rawlins is the associate provost for administration at Washington State University. In addition to his academic duties he was a research associate with the Brookings Institution from 1977 to 1979 and with the Woodrow Wilson School of Public and International Affairs at Princeton University from 1979 to 1983. He holds a Bachelors degree from Brigham Young University and a Doctorate in economics from the University of California, Berkeley.

Foreword

The idea that governments should create jobs for the unemployed has been assailed in U.S. politics in recent years as unworkable and wasteful, if not downright un-American. The biggest domestic budget cut (outside of the welfare field) achieved by President Reagan in 1981, his first year in office, was due to the elimination of the public service employment program under the Comprehensive Employment and Training Act (CETA). The program had already been trimmed in the Carter years from its post-recession peak in fiscal year 1979 of $4.1 billion on an annual basis. Hardly a murmur of dissent was heard in 1981 when the public service employment program was eliminated; CETA was described in this period by one critic as a "four-letter word," having the obvious connotation that one should not use it in polite society.

In light of this history, it is noteworthy that this book, culminating five years of research on the CETA public service jobs program, has good things to say about the program, rebutting some of the most common broadside criticisms. The book is based on field research in 40 state and local governmental jurisdictions and related studies. The research, conducted initially at the Brookings Institution, was completed at the Woodrow Wilson School of Public and International Affairs of Princeton University. This volume brings together for the first time the findings of all four rounds of field research conducted in July 1977, December 1977, December 1979 and December 1980. The sample included 40 jurisdictions covered by one or more field associate. The field researchers, mostly academic social scientists based at universities located in the jurisdictions being studied, collected program and budget data from a wide range of sources and conducted extensive interviews. Their findings, as summarized here by Robert F. Cook, Charles F. Adams, Jr., and V. Lane Rawlins, show that the CETA public service jobs program *worked*—and, in fact, worked well—during the 1976-78 period when there was "a good pool of trainees, real and important jobs to be learned, and employers who cared about getting the workers trained." Displacement (that is, the use of CETA job funds to pay for jobs that would have existed anyway) was found to be relatively low in this period.

The authors of this volume conclude further that a public service jobs program narrowly targeted on the most disadvantaged workers, which is what the program was modified to do in 1978, was not an effective strategy, primarily because employers (state and local governments and nonprofit organizations) no longer had as much incentive to make "good" use of the program for "real" jobs. The research in this case draws heavily on the *institutional* analyses by the field researchers, which are effectively integrated with impact analyses based both on field and statistical research techniques.

We need to pay close attention to these results in the current period. Although most observers of the domestic policy scene (even close observers) will tell you that the public service jobs approach was discredited and has been abandoned, there is, in effect, a new form of public service employment today focused on disadvantaged workers in the form of the "workfare" approach to welfare reform. This "work-for-your-welfare" idea was adopted by the Congress on a trial basis for the Aid to Families with Dependent Chidren (AFDC) program in 1981 at the request of President Reagan. This job-oriented approach to welfare reform is currently being tested in more than half of the states (generally limited to selected counties). It already shows promise as a basic institutional reform strategy for the welfare system (i.e., to make the system more strongly oriented to employment, self-sufficiency, and skill acquisition and enhancement). As we experiment with this employment and training approach to welfare reform, we will be well advised to pay close attention to the experience of earlier programs, including the mammoth CETA public service jobs program of the seventies ably described in this volume.

Richard P. Nathan

San Francisco, California
August 10, 1985

Preface

This book draws together research findings on the implementation and impact of public service employment as a major part of the nation's employment and training policy from 1971 to 1982.

The concept of public service employment can be simply stated. A significant number of people for one reason or another have a hard time finding jobs in private firms. One way the federal government can alleviate the problem of unemployment is to subsidize positions that these people can fill in state and local governments. This approach not only helps the previously unemployed gain skills and experience that may enable them to obtain unsubsidized employment, but also helps participating governments provide useful services for their citizens.

Though the concept in these bare essentials is fairly simple, those who legislate and implement a public service jobs program must confront a large number of complex issues. One overriding issue is the determination of program objectives and what relative weight each will have. Other issues include how money will be distributed, what kinds of people will be eligible for subsidized jobs, what restrictions will be imposed on participating government agencies in their use of subsidized workers, how much workers can be paid, and so on. During the decade that public service employment was emphasized in employment policy, more than one approach was tried for practically every aspect of the program's design. A basic purpose of this volume is to show how these various approaches affected the outcomes of the program.

The analysis presented here is based primarily on a longitudinal field evaluation study of 40 local governments and their implementation of the public service employment (PSE) component of the Comprehensive Employment and Training Act of 1973 (CETA). These field studies began in 1977, in response to a congressional mandate that the National Commission on Employment Policy sponsor a study of the "net employment effects" of the PSE program. The question that Congress was interested in at the time was how many PSE jobs were newly created positions, as Congress had intended, rather than simply federally subsidized replacements for positions that local governments would otherwise have funded with their own money. Later phases of the research considered a wide range of topics in addition to the net employment question.

The studies were undertaken by the Brookings Institution and later transferred to the Woodrow Wilson School of Public and International Affairs at Princeton University. At both Brookings and Princeton, the research was directed by Richard P. Nathan. The project resulted in four

vii

major reports submitted to the U.S. Department of Labor, as well as several other published works by project staff.

Field Evaluation Methodology

The PSE program was designed in Washington but implemented in hundreds of localities around the country. Any effort to understand how it operated and what effects it had must assemble and analyze evidence gathered at the local level to draw valid general conclusions that apply to the entire nation. It was with such requirements in mind that the field evaluation methodology was designed.

This approach has been used for studies of two other programs of federal grants to states and local governments—General Revenue Sharing and Community Development Block Grants.[1] These two research projects as well as the PSE study used a network of "field associates," who are economists or political scientists at universities or research institutions in the areas of the jurisdictions to be studied. Each field associate is a specialist in some aspect of intergovernmental grant research, such as labor economics, state and local finance, public administration, or intergovernmental relations. Each is also familiar with the operation of the program under study in the jurisdiction he or she reports on. As a result, the field associates are conversant with both the national policy questions related to the study and the local operation of the program under examination.

The field associates work in conjunction with the central staff of the project. For each field observation, the associates and the central staff meet to reach a common understanding of what issues are to be addressed and what types of information are needed. On the basis of this understanding, the central staff draws up a report form to guide the associates in their work. The form is neither an interview protocol nor a survey of responses of particular local actors. Rather, it is an outline of the questions that each associate must answer on the basis of the information he or she has gathered. Each associate is responsible for identifying the persons who should be interviewed and the other sources of information that should be used. Although members of the central staff may ask for clarifications and additional information, the analysis of the local situation is the responsibility of each associate.

After the central staff has received completed report forms from all associates and has obtained needed clarifications, members of the central staff (often in conjunction with some of the field associates) draft a report that attempts to generalize from the individual associate reports. All field associates have a chance to offer comments on this draft, and it is then revised and submitted as a product of the study.

Four rounds of observations were performed in the PSE study—in July 1977, December 1977, December 1979, and December 1980. Approximately 40 associates, covering 40 state and local jurisdictions, were involved in the study.

The Goal of This Report

Public policy sometimes goes in cycles. A political consensus is reached that "government should do something" about a social or economic problem. A program is devised to deal with the problem. After a time, the program comes to an end. When a similar problem later arises, all too often a brand new solution is devised, with little or no reference to the lessons that can be learned from the past.

Policymakers seeking to confront the problems of today typically fail to consult the nation's "institutional memory" about the policy initiatives of yesterday because of misperceptions about what those programs actually accomplished. When employment and training programs of the 1960s and 1970s were being designed, for example, hardly anyone fully appreciated the scope of the contributions that the work programs of the 1930s had made to American life. The Works Progress Administration produced a series of volumes on the economic history of major American rivers, but it failed to produce a contemporary record of the hundreds of projects it supported. As a result, the public memory of such programs was shrouded in political rhetoric, much of it condemning them as "make work." Yet their accomplishments—aside from protecting millions of American families from destitution—were real and lasting, as anyone can attest who has visited one of the thousands of public libraries built by WPA workers, flown into LaGuardia Airport in New York City, also built by WPA workers, or hiked in state parks that were reforested by the Civilian Conservation Corps.

Although the public service employment program came to an end only a few years ago, we believe it has already met a fate similar to that of the Depression-era programs. We believe there is a need to go beyond the contemporary rhetoric and provide a dispassionate assessment of the strengths and weaknesses of this program. If the need for subsidized public service jobs should again arise, as we believe it may, the record will be available to those who care to learn from it.

NOTE

1. See Richard P. Nathan et al., *Monitoring Revenue Sharing* (Washington, DC: The Brookings Institution, 1975); Richard P. Nathan, Charles F. Adams, Jr., and Associates, *Revenue Sharing: The Second Round* (Brookings, 1977); and Paul R. Dommel et al., *Targeting Community Development* (Washington, DC: U.S. Department of Housing and Urban Development, 1980). For details on the field evaluation method, see Richard P. Nathan, "The Methodology for Field Network Evaluation Studies," in Walter Williams, ed., *Studying Implementation* (Chatham, NJ: Chatham House, 1982).

Field Research Associates

Associates	Sites
Charles F. Adams, Jr. Ohio State University with the assistance of Glen Hahn	Franklin County, Ohio
James Austin and Janet M. Galchick Princeton University	Mercer County, New Jersey
Roger Bowlby University of Tennessee	Knoxville, Tennessee
Joseph M. Davis and Patricia Barry Federation for Community Planning	Cleveland, Ohio
John M. Degrove Florida Atlantic- International University and Deborah Athos State of Florida	Seminole County, Florida
Steven M. Director Rutgers University	Morristown, New Jersey Parsippany-Troy Hills Twp., New Jersey
Frederick C. Doolittle Harvard University	Boston, Massachusetts
William O. Farber University of South Dakota	Minnehaha County, South Dakota Rapid City, South Dakota
Patricia Florestano University of Maryland	Baltimore, Maryland
John S. Hall Arizona State University	Maricopa County, Arizona Phoenix, Arizona

H. Allan Hunt
W.E. Upjohn Institute
for Employment Research
with Jo Bentley Reece

Cass County, Michigan
Van Buren County, Michigan

John S. Jackson, III
Southern Illinois University

Shawnee Consortium, Illinois

James E. Jernberg
University of Minnesota

St. Paul, Minnesota

Morris M. Kleiner
University of Kansas

Atchison County, Kansas

David R. Knowles
Seattle University

Grays Harbor County,
Washington
Kitsap County, Washington

Geraldine Larkin
Ann Arbor, Michigan

Detroit, Michigan

Sarah F. Liebschutz
and
Edward H. Downey
State University of New York,
Brockport

Rochester, New York

William H. Lucy
University of Virginia

Charlottesville, Virginia

Susan A. MacManus
University of Houston

Houston, Texas

Mark Morlock
California State University,
Chico

Eugene, Oregon
Lane County, Oregon

Charles J. Orlebeke
University of Illinois,
Chicago Circle

Chicago, Illinois

Kenneth Palmer
and
James F. Horan
University of Maine

Bangor, Maine
Portland, Maine

Maureen Pirog-Good
University of Pennsylvania
with the assistance of
Janice Shack

Philadelphia, Pennsylvania

Ruth Ross
  California State University,
  Long Beach

Thomas N. Schaap
  Clemson University
  and
Rodney M. Mabry
  Northeast Louisiana University

Lewis H. Smith
  University of Mississippi

Steve B. Steib
  and
Lynn Rittenoure
  University of Tulsa

Eugene F. Wagner
  University of Missouri
  at Kansas City

William D. Wagoner,
Emil Meurer, and
Marcia Verret
  University of New Orleans

George D. Wendel
  and
E. Allan Tomey
  St. Louis University

Michael L. Wiseman
  University of California,
  Berkeley
  with the assistance of
  Sandra Threlfall

El Monte, California
Los Angeles, California

Anderson County,
South Carolina

Pickens County,
South Carolina

Lowndes County, Mississippi

Tulsa, Oklahoma

Independence, Missouri
Kansas City, Missouri

Jefferson Parish, Louisiana
New Orleans, Louisiana

St. Louis, Missouri
University City, Missouri

San Francisco, California

Contents

1
The Public Service Employment Program

At various times during the 1970s, public service job programs were seen by various people as a solution to long term unemployment among technologically displaced and/or unskilled people, as a strategy to combat short term unemployment caused by economic downturns, as an alternative to welfare, and as a scandal-ridden failure.

The programs were none of these things, yet each view has an element of truth. Public service jobs programs could be viewed from many different perspectives for two main reasons. First, they had multiple objectives, and different observers could judge the programs by different criteria. Second, the programs were undergoing almost continuous change. Information gathered in one year might not apply to the program in the following year.

This chapter describes the objectives and design of the Public Employment Program (PEP) of 1971 and its successor, the Public Service Employment (PSE) components of the Comprehensive Employment and Training Act of 1973 (CETA). It begins by sketching the background to these programs, as set in the 1930s and 1960s.

Background

The Works Progress Administration (WPA), begun in 1935 as one of Franklin D. Roosevelt's responses to the Great Depression, established the precedent of direct federal government involvement in countering widespread unemployment. At its peak, it employed more than 3 million people while more than 9 million were unemployed. It distributed an average of $1.4 billion per year until its end in 1943.[1]

Partly because WPA set a precedent by involving the federal government in efforts to directly reduce unemployment, it was a controversial program. Its opponents castigated it as "leaf raking" and "the dole," but since that time many have come to appreciate the amount of productive output the program supported.[2]

Despite its obvious similarities to the public service employment programs of the 1970s, WPA differed from them in two important respects. First, its primary objective was to replace household income lost when a breadwinner was laid off. (Unemployment compensation was not provided nationwide until 1938.) Only one worker in a family could hold a WPA job; workers did not receive ordinary wages, but were given an amount equal to the difference between any other income and what the government determined to be their "need." Second, WPA was administered directly by the federal government, with a federal administrator in each locality, rather than by state or local governments.

Programs of the 1960s

Mobilization for World War II eliminated the unemployment problem of the depression, and for a decade after the war joblessness was not a major issue. The government provided a year's worth of unemployment compensation to returning vetrans; a business boom absorbed civilians thrown out of work in defense industries; and the Korean War, which began in 1950, ended a mild recession that had started in late 1948. The end of the Korean conflict in 1953 brought a downturn, but it turned out to be brief.[3]

Calls for government efforts to stimulate the economy and create jobs began to be heard, however, when a sluggish economy from 1957 through 1960 brought persistently high unemployment levels. Further impetus for action arose from concerns that many people would be thrown out of work by the effects of automation resulting from the technological advances of the previous two decades.

Soon after the Kennedy administration took office, Congress in 1961 approved the Area Redevelopment Act. It combined loans and other incentives for firms to expand industrial facilities in economically depressed areas with vocational education programs intended to assure industries of a trained workforce in those areas. With a new economic downturn in 1961, however, the program proved to be too small to create many jobs, and the training component never exceeded 12,000 persons through the program's end in 1965.

A much more ambitious effort began in 1962, when the Kennedy administration won passage of the Manpower Development and Training Act (MDTA). It focused on training, especially the retraining of workers whose skills did not fit the changing needs of the economy. The largest part of the training was done by educational institutions and local community agencies; the number of persons receiving such training rose from 32,000 in fiscal year 1963 to a peak of 177,500 in fiscal year 1966. The program also made an effort to place unemployed people in jobs with private firms where they could receive on-the-job training. The firms were given subsidies to cover the extra costs of hiring unskilled workers. Private social action organizations received grants to find firms that were willing to participate. This portion of the MDTA program grew at first, but the Johnson administration's 1964 declaration of a War on Poverty gave MDTA a new focus on the poor rather than the more general mandate to meet the training needs of the unskilled and technologically displaced.

The opening salvo of the war on poverty came with the passage of the Economic Opportunity Act of 1964. This act and its subsequent amendments brought about an explosion of new training programs, each designed for a particular segment of the poverty population. Following are the major categories of people and the programs designed to help them gain skills and jobs:

- *Welfare Recipients:* One of the nation's most vexing problems of the sixties was the growing number of households dependent on Aid to Families with Dependent Children (AFDC). In 1962, a two-year experiment called the Community Work and Training Program offered work experience to AFDC recipients. This was expanded in 1964 into the Work Experience Program (later renamed the Work Experience and Training Program). This effort evolved in 1967 into the Work Incentive Program (WIN), with the Department of Health and Human Services providing such support services as medical care and child day care, and the Department of Labor providing training and job placement for women receiving AFDC with children above age six.

- *Youths:* The Job Corps set up residential centers, often in rural areas, for young people from inner cities, providing them with remedial education and job skills training. The Neighborhood Youth Corps, which operated in the cities where youths lived, provided part-time work experience, remedial education, and limited job training for high school dropouts and potential dropouts.

- *Rural Elderly:* Operation Mainstream provided work experience and income maintenance for workers over fifty-five in rural areas, where job opportunities are particularly scarce.

- *Disadvantaged Adults and Out-of-School Youths:* The New Careers Program was begun in 1966 to train paraprofessionals in such public service fields as health, education, welfare, neighborhood redevelopment, and public safety. It was subsumed and expanded in 1970 by the Public Service Careers Program, which added an effort to facilitate placement and eliminate barriers to employment.

The federal government has also made efforts to involve private firms in programs to train the unemployed and create jobs for them. The Job Opportunities in the Business Sector (JOBS) program, started in 1967, was a joint effort of the public and private sectors to develop on-the-job training programs for the disadvantaged. Later, tax credits were offered to firms that hired people who were eligible for job training programs. Relatively few employers used this tax credit, however, and a General Accounting Office study found that about 70 percent of the workers for whom tax credits had been granted were already employed prior to the credit allowance. The Economic Recovery Tax Act of 1981 included provisions to restrict credits to newly hired employees.

The Public Employment Program

Although the programs of the 1960s were numerous, they did not involve the federal government in providing subsidized public service jobs. The idea of doing so was considered in 1969 when recession put an end to the prosperity of the previous decade. Congress responded by passing a general public employment program in 1970, but President Nixon vetoed it. The following year, when the unemployment rate reached a peak of 6 percent (a high figure for the time), Congress and the president reached agreement on another bill: the Emergency Employment Act of 1971, which authorized the Public Employment Program (PEP).

PEP was considered a pilot program, and was intended to last only two years. It was, however, a sizable effort to counter cyclical unemployment. Funding was $1 billion for fiscal year 1972 and $1.25 billion for 1973. At its peak in July 1972, it provided employment for about 185,000 persons.[4]

In keeping with the Nixon administration's philosophy of "New Federalism"—that is, increasing the role of state and local governments in the operation of social programs that had previously been operated primarily by the federal government—PEP put responsibility for operations in the hands of state and local governments. Funds went to states and to municipalities or counties serving populations of 75,000 or more. The bulk of the money was allocated to governments in areas with unemployment rates higher than 4.5 percent; additional money was distributed to areas with rates of 6 percent or more.

The federal government imposed very few restrictions on the state and local governments receiving funds. They could hire anyone who had been out of work for a week or more (later changed to two weeks), or who was underemployed. Underemployment was defined as working less than full time involuntarily, or working full time at wages that provided less than a poverty-level income. Preference was to be given to Vietnam veterans, youths and older workers, migrants, workers who did not speak English, welfare recipients, disadvantaged persons, and displaced scientists and engineers. Such broad "targeting" amounts to none at all. With so few rules, the federal government in effect "put the money on the stump and ran," a characterization of many of the intergovernmental grant initiatives of this period. This approach followed the philosophy of the early New Federalism, and was close to the design of the general revenue sharing program, passed in 1972. The approach did, however, enable participating governments to hire subsidized workers quickly, which was a primary goal of the program.

State and local governments naturally tended to hire workers who fit easily into established workforce patterns. Large percentages of participants were white (64 percent), male (72 percent), and between the ages of 22 and 44 (64 percent). Forty-three percent had gone to school through twelfth grade, and another 31 percent had education after high school.[5] PEP participants were better educated and less disadvantaged than participants in the more structurally oriented programs begun in the sixties, and fewer were minorities.

Although the act authorized training, little money was spent for this purpose; an estimated 94 percent of the money was spent on compensation of participants.[6] The state and local governments that directly received PEP funds could subcontract to other units of governments, but little of this was done. Although data were not collected on this point, probably no more than 10 percent of the positions were subcontracted, and those were mostly to independent school districts.

Start and Growth
of Public Service Employment

PEP was an addition to the collection of training programs that preceded it, not a replacement. These older programs, which had various clienteles and different operating organizations, were criticized for being uncoordinated and sometimes duplicative. Partly in response to this concern and partly in response to the Nixon administration's continued support of the concept of New Federalism, Congress in 1973 passed the Comprehensive Employment and Training Act (CETA).

As originally passed, CETA had three main components. First, Title I established a formula to distribute money for training programs to state and local governments, and gave these governments the power to determine what particular kinds of programs they would operate. The state or local governments that received the funds directly, called "prime sponsors," could choose which agencies—public or nonprofit—would run the training programs. Second, Title II established a relatively small public service employment program that would operate in areas of "substantial unemployment," defined as unemployment of 6.5 percent or more.

The initial appropriation for Title II was $370 million; an additional $250 million was allocated to phase out PEP until July 1974, when Title II took over. Finally, Title III allowed for direct federal operation of some national training programs aimed at special groups, such as Indians, migrants, and youths, and Title IV continued the Job Corps.

Title II was primarily designed to combat structural unemployment; the need for a program to alleviate cyclical joblessness was not strongly felt in 1973, since the peak of unemployment associated with the recession of 1969-71 had passed two years earlier. Those eligible for jobs under Title II were those who had been unemployed for 30 days or more, or were underemployed.

No sooner had programs started operating under Title II in the summer of 1974, however, than the nation began to suffer another major recession, this one largely brought on by sharply rising energy costs associated with the Arab oil embargo. Unemployment rose rapidly, eventually reaching a peak of 8.7 percent in the spring of 1975. In December 1974, Congress reacted to the joblessness problem by passing the Emergency Jobs and Unemployment Assistance Act of 1974, which added Title VI to CETA. Title VI established a PSE program that was explicitly countercyclical. Funds were to be given to prime sponsors in all areas. To be eligible for a Title VI job, a person had to be unemployed for 30 days, or for 15 days if the local unemployment rate was more than 7 percent. Originally authorized for just 18 months, Title VI began with an appropriation of $875 million.

Implementation of Title VI brought rapid growth to the PSE program. As of December 1974, about 56,000 people were enrolled in Title II. Grants under Title VI went out to prime sponsors starting in January 1975, and by the end of June 1975 enrollments stood at about 155,000 for Title II and 125,000 for Title VI. The total enrollment in public service jobs programs (including participants in the PEP program's final months) stood at 310,000 in May 1975.[7] Figure

1-1 shows the changes in enrollment levels in the various programs and titles over the decade.

The rapid buildup of Title VI enrollments strongly affected the nature of the PSE program in its early months, as well as perceptions of it in Congress. The emphasis during this period was on hiring participants quickly to combat the effects of the recession. As had happened earlier with PEP, state and local governments were quickest to hire participants with good educational and work backgrounds. As a result, the first report on the characteristics of PSE participants, based on a sample taken between January and March 1975, showed that large proportions were white (66 percent), male (71 percent), of prime working age (63 percent between ages 22 and 44), well educated (76 percent had 12 years of schooling or more), and not economically disadvantaged (64 percent).[8]

These figures made the initial group of PSE participants look quite similar to regular employees of state and local governments. This perception, in combination with a Labor Department paper from 1974 suggesting, in theory, that PSE might have the effect of displacing many locally paid workers with federally subsidized workers,[9] led many in Congress to conclude that such displacement was in fact happening on a large scale.

This conclusion led to the first of several major congressionally-mandated shifts in the design of the PSE program. Title VI was due to expire on June 30, 1976. Unemployment remained relatively high—it averaged 7.7 percent during 1976—so as that date drew closer there was considerable pressure for renewing the title. The Senate, however, refused to approve a new Title VI authorization until changes were made. A stopgap appropriation in April carried Title VI participants on the Title II payroll until new legislation could be worked out. On October 1, 1976, Congress passed the Emergency Jobs Program Extension Act, providing new funds for Title VI, retroactive to June 30.

Figure 1-1
Enrollments in Titles II and VI
and Total PSE, by Quarter
September 1971 to September 1981

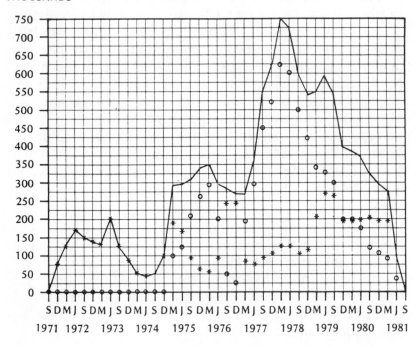

THOUSANDS

S DM J S DM J S DM J S DM J S DM J S DM J S DM J S DM J S DM J S DM J S
1971 1972 1973 1974 1975 1976 1977 1978 1979 1980 1981

MONTH AND YEAR

LEGEND

——— = Total Enrollments

∘∘∘∘ = Title VI Enrollments

**** = Title II Enrollments

S = September, D = December, M = March, J = June

NOTE: PEP enrollments are included in Title II enrollment figures through June 1976.

The new legislation made two major changes in Title VI:

1. It required that all newly-hired Title VI workers beyond the number needed to "sustain" state and local governments at their previous level of PSE workers be assigned to special projects that would last for no more than a year. In effect, the PSE program now consisted of two components: "sustainment" positions, funded under Title II and part of the Title VI appropriation, and "project" positions, funded with the rest of the Title VI appropriation.

2. The act also imposed new restrictions on eligibility. Half of the vacancies arising under the sustainment portion of all the new positions created under the project portion were to be filled with people who had been unemployed for at least 15 out of the preceding 20 weeks. The previous rule required no more than 30 days of unemployment.

The idea behind the "projects" approach was to remove PSE employees from the regular operation of the state or local government. The one-year projects were supposed to consist of specific tasks that would not otherwise be performed. The result, Congress hoped, would be to make displacement more difficult. The new eligibility rules were intended to target the program on the long term unemployed and on low-income people. (The rules also stated that during the previous three months, participants had to earn no more than 70 percent of the "lower living standard" set by the Bureau of Labor Statistics. However, people who met the unemployment criterion generally also met the income criterion.)

Although Title VI was supposed to be the countercyclical element of PSE, the 1976 amendments gave it eligibility rules more appropriate to a structural program aimed at the long term unemployed while leaving Title II, the original structural element, with rules more appropriate for a countercyclical program. The net effect of the changes, however, was to shift the overall PSE program to a greater structural emphasis. Even though the amendments allowed prime sponsors to fill half of the sustainment vacancies with people who met the old eligibility rule, in practice most prime sponsors applied the new rule to all new participants. This practice allowed program operators to shift participants from one title to another if funding levels for the two titles changed substantially, as had happened in 1976 while Title VI was temporarily suspended.

The 1977 Buildup

In May 1977, shortly after President Carter took office, Congress passed his administration's economic stimulus program designed to provide jobs in the midst of continuing economic stagnation. An additional $4 billion was pumped into PSE for 1977 and 1978, much of it going to Title VI projects. Enrollment in the two titles rose rapidly, from roughly 300,000 in May 1977 to a peak of 755,000 in April 1978.

During this period, prime sponsors increased the number of PSE positions that were subcontracted to community-based organizations. The 1976 amendments to the act recommended that a "substantial" portion of PSE funds be channeled to such groups; the Department of Labor later defined "substantial" as one-third of the positions.[10] When the Brookings field evaluation team made its first observation in July 1977, it found that 10 percent of the sustainment positions and almost one-fourth of the project positions were subcontracted to nonprofit organizations.[11] By the time of the second observation in December 1977, when total enrollment stood at 610,000, one-fourth of all participants were assigned to work in nonprofit organizations; the proportion for "sustainment" positions was 10 percent, and for the "project" portion 43 percent.[12]

The 1978 Amendments

In October 1978, Congress made further substantial changes to the PSE program when it passed new legislation reauthorizing CETA. Eligibility rules were again tightened, requiring applicants to have been unemployed for 15 weeks in the case of Title II or 10 weeks for Title VI (see table 1-1). Limits were tightened on the amount PSE workers could be paid, and new limits were imposed on the length of time any worker could remain in the program. These changes were designed to focus the program on the long term unemployed and to further limit prime sponsors' ability to displace regular workers with PSE workers.

Just as important, Congress required prime sponsors to set aside a certain percentage of funds to provide formal training for PSE participants. Helping state and local governments provide services was no longer one of the objectives of PSE. This goal, in fact, was no longer mentioned in the law. Instead, the primary focus was now on training the unemployed who had low levels of skills.

As it turned out, 1978 was the beginning of the end for PSE. The shift in goals mandated by the congressional amendments made local governments less enthusiastic about participating in the program, as chapter 2 will explain. Talk in the Carter administration of converting PSE into a welfare reform program cast further doubt on the ability of local officials to meet service goals through PSE; proposed was a "Better Jobs and Income Program" that would have provided minimum-wage public service jobs to heads of households receiving public assistance, and would have been administered through prime sponsors by the federal government.

Enrollments in PSE dropped by 150,000 between September 1978 and August 1979. When the limits on the amount of time a person could stay in the program began to have an effect in September 1979, program operators began to terminate participants and not replace them. This brought enrollments down by another 150,000. Funding for PSE dropped from $4.1 billion in fiscal year 1979 to $3.2 billion in fiscal year 1980.

Table 1-1
Summary of Legislative Changes in Public Service Employment

Public employment program	Original CETA Legislation, 1973	
	Title II	Title VI
Eligibility Unemployed or underemployed persons	Participants must (1) reside in an area of substantial unemployment *and* (2) be unemployed at least 30 days before application, or be underemployed.	Unemployed for 30 days (15 days in areas of substantial unemployment) or be underemployed.
Training Up to 15 percent of the funds could be used for training and supportive services.	No requirement	No requirement
Duration No limit	No limit	No limit
Wages No limit on wages or local supplements. Limit of $10,000 annually in federally funded wages.	*Maximum* of $10,000 annually to any participant. Employers *may supplement* wages with own funds. Labor Department may ''make general recommendations to prime sponsors'' in effort to keep national average to $7,800.	Maximum of $10,000 annually with a national average of $7,800 per participant.

| | 1976 amendments | 1978 amendments | |
	Title VI projects	Title II-D	Title VI
	Half of "sustainment" participants must be unemployed 30 days before application (15 days in areas of high unemployment). Other half of "sustainment" participants must (1) have low income (defined as 70 percent of lower living standard) and (2) be unemployed for at least 15 weeks or receiving AFDC.	Participants must (1) be unemployed at least 15 weeks and be economically disadvantaged, or (2) receive Aid to Families with Dependent Children or Supplemental Security Income benefits.	Participants must (1) be unemployed at time of determination and for at least 10 of the previous 12 weeks, and (2) have low income (defined as 100 percent of lower living standard) or receive AFDC or SSI.
	No requirement	At least 15 percent of funds should be used for classroom training or individual instruction. Informal on-the-job training does not count.	At least 5 percent of Title VI funds should be used for training, counseling, and services to participants.
	No individual limit. Projects were to last no more than 12 months.	Participants limited to maximum 18 months in PSE out of a 5-year period. Labor Department may grant waivers for up to 12 months over limit to jurisdictions with at least 7 percent unemployment rate and "unusually severe hardship" in shifting participants to unsubsidized jobs.	Same as Title II.
	Essentially same as Title II	*Maximum* $10,000 can be adjusted to as high as $12,000 for high-wage areas. Employers *may not supplement* wages of those hired after 9/30/78. National *average* should be $7,600. Average wage in individual jurisdictions is adjusted according to a geographic wage index.	Maximum and average limits same as Title II.

The end of PSE came in 1981, when the Reagan administration took office. Citing continuing charges of fraud and abuse by local governments, the high cost per participant, and low rates of placement in unsubsidized jobs as reported by prime sponsors, the administration persuaded Congress to rescind the program's spending authority for fiscal year 1981 and to eliminate any authorization for fiscal year 1982. As a result, PSE ended on September 30, 1981.

The primary vehicle for job training became the Job Training Partnership Act (JTPA), which replaced CETA as of October 1, 1983. Unlike CETA, JTPA does not channel federal money directly to local governments; instead, funds go to each state governor, for allocation within the state. Also, JTPA puts a much heavier emphasis than CETA did on cooperation with the private sector. (The principal mechanism for such interaction under CETA had been Title VII.) At the local level, each area's JTPA program is run under an agreement between local government and a Private Industry Council (PIC), which includes a majority of representatives from private business. JTPA programs focus on training; they can include little work experience or payment of stipends to participants. JTPA explicitly prohibits public service employment. Finally, JTPA contains a component to retrain dislocated workers—that is, experienced workers who have lost jobs in declining industries or whose skills have become obsolete because of technological advances. This final aspect of JTPA is quite similar to the emphasis in the Manpower Development and Training Act of 1962, where large-scale federal training efforts had their start in the postwar era.

CETA Title II

Purpose

The legislative statement of purpose for the original Title II was the same as for PEP; it emphasized transitional employment and the provision of needed public services.

Eligibility

To be eligible for Title II, a person had to reside in an area of substantial unemployment and have been unemployed for 30 days or be underemployed. Significant segments of the population that were to be given equitable treatment were the long term unemployed, Vietnam veterans, AFDC recipients, and former employment and training program participants.

Types of Jobs

Sponsors were to establish a goal of limiting participation in PSE to 12 months. Sponsors were required to pay wages comparable to unsubsidized workers in similar jobs. A maximum wage of $10,000 was continued, along with an average wage of $7,800. There was no limit on the extent to which local sponsors could supplement the PSE wage. There were also no restrictions on the types of jobs that Title II participants could hold.

Training

No less than 90 percent of the funds were to be used for wages; the remaining funds were to be used for administration, training, and supportive services. Given the small percentage of funds involved, administration took precedence over training.

CETA Title VI

Purpose

Same as Title II.

Eligibility

To be eligible, participants had to have been unemployed for at least 30 days or be underemployed. If they lived in an area of excess unemployment (having an unemployment rate of 7 percent for three consecutive months), they had to have been unemployed for 15 days. Special attention was to be given to persons who had been unemployed for 15 weeks or more, those who had exhausted their unemployment benefits, and those who were unemployed but not eligible for unemployment benefits. Also to receive special consideration were welfare recipients, veterans, and former employment and training participants.

Types of Jobs

Employing agencies were required to pay wages comparable to prevailing rates for other jobs with the same employer. Wages were limited to a maximum of $10,000 per year, with a $7,800 national average. With regard to the types of jobs that could be held, individuals were to be employed in projects with a duration of 12 months or less, although there was no limit on the duration of tenure in the PSE jobs.

Training and Transition

Ninety percent of the funds were to be used for wages and benefits. The remaining 10 percent included administration, leaving little for training and support services. Sponsors were to place 50 percent of their participants, but this was only a goal and waivers were readily accepted.

Title VI Projects

Purpose

To sustain the PSE jobs under Titles II and VI that existed as of June 1976 and require that any jobs above that level be used in projects of short duration.

Eligibility

Half of the vacancies in the existing "sustainment" Title VI and all additional participants had to meet the new eligibility requirements. People filling these vacancies had to (1) have a family income in the preceding three months that was at or below 70 percent of the BLS lower living standard, and (2) be unemployed for 15 weeks or have exhausted their unemployment benefits, or be in a family that was receiving AFDC benefits. This had the effect of requiring both a history of unemployment and low household income, though the income requirement was diluted somewhat by limiting it to three months prior to application, the same period as the unemployment requirement.

Types of Jobs

Participants were to be employed in projects of a one-time nature that had a duration of 12 months or less. In addition, a "substantial portion" of these jobs were to be in nonprofit organizations.[15]

Training

Eighty-five percent of the funds were to be used for wages and benefits, the rest being used for administration. There was no rule that agents set aside any share of the funds for training or support services.

Title II-D

Purpose

With the reauthorization of CETA in October 1978, the purpose of Title II was amended to include training and related services to enable participants to move into unsubsidized employment or training. Title II-D was now to be a structural program.

Eligibility

Eligibility was tightened considerably to require that an individual be economically disadvantaged and unemployed for 15 of the prior 20 weeks or be a member of a family that was receiving public assistance. "Economically disadvantaged" meant a family income less than or equal to 70 percent of the BLS lower living standard. Households with a governmentally supported foster child, a handicapped person, or a patient or outpatient of a prison, hospital, or community care facility could also be considered economically disadvantaged. Preference was to be given to the long term unemployed, public assistance recipients, disabled and Vietnam-era veterans, persons with limited English-speaking ability, the handicapped, women, single parent, displaced homemakers, youth, older workers, and individuals with limited education (a fairly impressive list).

Types of Jobs

The jobs provided were to be entry level, combined with training and support services, and designed to enable participants to move into unsubsidized employment. Project jobs were not required to be entry level. Tenure in the program was limited to 18 months in any five-year period.[16] Wages were limited to a maximum of $10,000 and an average of $7,200, both adjusted by an area wage index within the range of 110 percent of the poverty line to 120 percent of the maximum wage. No local supplementation of wage levels in Title II-D was allowed.

Training

Ten percent of the funds were to be used for training in fiscal year 1979, 15 percent in fiscal year 1980, and 20 percent in fiscal year 1981.

Post-1978 Title VI

Purpose

With the reauthorization of CETA in 1978, Congress tried to convert Title VI back to a strictly countercyclical program. That title was now to provide "temporary employment during periods of high unemployment" and funding was to be geared to the level of national unemployment, providing jobs for 20 percent of the unemployed if the national unemployment rate was more than 4 percent. If the national unemployment rate was in excess of 7 percent, the program was to employ 25 percent of the unemployed in excess of 4 percent of the labor force. Note that the provision of public services was no longer a stated purpose of Title VI.

Eligibility

To be eligible, participants had to have been unemployed for at least 10 of the preceding 12 weeks, be currently unemployed, and be from a family that had an income less than or equal to the BLS lower living standard or that was receiving public assistance. The same groups were given preference as under Title II-D.

Types of Jobs

Half of the jobs were to be entry-level public service jobs. The other half were to be in projects with a planned duration of 18 months or less. One-third of the funds was to be used to support jobs in the nonprofit sector. Wages were limited to $10,000. This maximum was adjusted by up to 20 percent, based on the wage index for the area. Average wages were to be $7,200, again adjusted for the wage index of the area. Local supplementation of wages was limited to 10 percent of the funds under Title VI or 20 percent of the maximum in the case of any individual participant.

Training

Not less than 10 percent of the funds in fiscal year 1979 and 5 percent or more of the funds in successive years was to be used for training. In addition, sponsors were to prepare employability development plans for participants and specify in their plans the rates of transition that they hoped to achieve.

NOTES

1. *Manpower Report of the President* (Washington, DC: U.S. Government Printing Office, 1975), p. 40.

2. Jonathan R. Kesselman, "Work Relief Programs in the Great Depression," in John L. Palmer, ed., *Creating Public Jobs: Public Employment Programs and Wage Subsidies* (Washington, DC: The Brookings Institution, 1978).

3. Much of this section is based on Ewan Clague and Leo Kramer, *Manpower Policies and Programs: A Review, 1935-75* (Kalamazoo, MI: W. E. Upjohn Institute, 1976).

4. Sar A. Levitan and Robert Taggart, *Emergency Employment Act: The PEP Generation* (Salt Lake City: Olympus, 1974), p. 12.

5. Levitan and Taggart, Table I-4, pp. 27-30.

6. Ibid., p. 16.

7. *Employment and Training Report of the President,* 1976, p. 97.

8. Westat, Inc., "Characteristics of CETA Participants Enrolled During Third Quarter of FY 1975," Continuous Longitudinal Manpower Survey Report No. 1 (Prepared for U.S. Department of Labor, January 1976), p. 1-4.

9. George E. Johnson, "Evaluation Questions Under the Comprehensive Employment and Training Act of 1973," Framework for Evaluation Paper No. 2, U.S. Department of Labor, Office of the Assistant Secretary for Policy, Evaluation, and Research, July 1974.

10. U.S. Department of Labor, Employment and Training Administration, Field Memorandum No. 316-77, June 17, 1977.

11. Richard P. Nathan et al., *Monitoring the Public Service Employment Program* (Washington, DC: National Commission for Manpower Policy, March 1978), Table 3-1, p. 33.

12. Richard P. Nathan et al., *Monitoring the Public Service Employment Program: The Second Round,* Special Report No. 32 (Washington, DC: National Commission for Manpower Policy, March 1979), p. 33.

13. Public law 92-54, section 2.

14. Public law 92-52, section 7 (c) (2).

15. "Substantial" was later defined (Field Memo 316 p. 77, issued June 17, 1977) as one-third of the funds. The wage limits remained the same as for the previous Title VI.

16. In the field evaluation, a number of associates noted that sponsors already had a limit of one year in PSE—presumably dating back to the goal stated in the original Title II.

2
How PSE Looked at the Local Level

The public service employment titles of CETA were expressions of federal policy, but this policy was implemented by state and local governments. This arrangement was one of the most important facts about the public service job programs of the 1970s and a major element that determined their outcomes.

If the objectives of the federal government had coincided with those of the governments that operated the programs, no issue would have arisen. But in fact local and state governments put primary weight on one objective—using PSE workers to help provide services—while the federal government focused on the objectives of creating jobs to ease cyclical unemployment and of providing work experience and training to the unskilled. PEP in 1971-73 and PSE in its first three years emphasized job creation, while PSE after 1976—and especially after 1978—emphasized training, but both objectives were found to some degree throughout the history of these two programs. For such programs to work, some sort of bargaining had to take place that resulted in a balance more or less satisfactory to both the federal government and the local program operators.

The story that emerges from the field research conducted at Brookings and Princeton is that such a balance was possible while the federal government's primary emphasis was on job creation. The relative lack of restrictions on local program operators allowed them to hire large numbers of people who needed little training to fill positions that provided valuable services. Once the federal emphasis shifted to training the unskilled, the balance became more difficult to maintain, and with the 1978 restrictions became nearly impossible. Whatever success PSE had after 1978 in providing work experience and training to the unskilled—and we will see in chapters 3 and 4 that it was not insubstantial—such accomplishments were costly in terms of local goals of providing services.

This chapter examines the relationship among the three objectives for public service employment, and shows how some of the outcomes of the program shifted with changes in federal government emphasis. These outcomes include the characteristics of the participants, the kinds of jobs they held, and the types of services they helped to provide. We also present evidence that different types of localities responded to the program changes in somewhat different ways, especially when localities that were in relatively good fiscal condition are compared with those that were not.

Local Objectives and Job Creation

During the period that job creation was uppermost in the minds of Congress and the federal administration, displacement was the most widely discussed issue related to local government use of public service employment funds. The fear held by many members of Congress, as noted in chapter 1, was that many local governments would simply switch the source of funding for large numbers of government positions from locally raised taxes to the federal PSE subsidy. If this were to happen, the total number of jobs in local government agencies would stay about the same—or, to put it another way, the "net employment effect" of the federal program would be minimal.

This fear was not entirely baseless. Many local governments were facing budget crises due to the economic downturns of 1969-70 and 1973-74 which made it difficult to continue providing services in the face of declining tax revenue. The situation was especially severe for many older large cities, where revenue problems were compounded by the departure of businesses to suburbs and to other regions of the country. Rather than raise local tax rates, such cities might have used PSE funds for fiscal relief.

As we will show in chapter 3, the amount of displacement found by the field associates was less than had been suggested by some observers. Nevertheless, the field associates did confirm that displacement was higher in large, distressed cities than in jurisdictions with less severe fiscal problems. More importantly, however, many of those governments were found to have used PSE funds to maintain positions that would have been eliminated without PSE; when elimination seemed to have been the only alternative, the field associates considered this use of PSE funds to be "program maintenance," rather than displacement.

Fraud and Abuse

An issue related to displacement is that of fraud and abuse. The PSE program acquired a reputation for fraud and abuse in its execution based largely on the wide publicity the news media gave to reports of improper or illegal use of PSE funds by local governments or other employing agencies.

The term "fraud and abuse" covers considerable territory with unclear boundaries. It can refer to plainly criminal actions such as bribe-taking, or to more subtle violations such as political favoritism in hiring actions and budget allocations. Because the popular perception of PSE is that corruption was endemic to the program, we considered it important to include in our third-round field report form an analysis of this topic. The associates were in no sense program auditors or investigators; they were asked only to note instances of fraud and abuse that had either been documented by official action such as an audit, or had been publicly alleged by newspapers, community organizations, civic groups, or aggrieved citizens. Such a survey does not provide a definitive picture, particularly because an allegation of abuse may itself turn out to be unfounded or politically motivated. Yet the survey has some use as a general indicator of the level of program abuses.

According to the associates' reports, three out of every five jurisdictions were "clean"; no instances of program misconduct had been documented or even alleged. About one-fifth (22 percent) of the jurisdictions were reported to have had isolated or minor abuses, such as misappropriation of a small amount of PSE funds by a single PSE official, or failure of an employing agency to carry out its contract.

Ten percent of the jurisdictions had been cited for program abuses. The main problem was the use of PSE for political patronage. These jurisdictions were ordered by the Department of Labor to take corrective action. In three jurisdictions, allegations of misconduct were being investigated at the time of the round three observation. Finally, there was one jurisdiction where multiple, recurring abuses formed a pattern of persistent maladministration. The associate for this jurisdiction cited such actions as irregular purchasing and contracting procedures, use of PSE funds for ineligible purposes, poor monitoring, use of PSE participants in political campaigns, and appointment of PSE staff based on political rather than professional qualifications.

The picture is not as consistently good as one would like, nor as bad as one could infer from the popular press. PSE has hardly been a model of purity; there have been enough PSE "horror stories" to prompt at least one writer to call CETA a "four-letter word."[1] Such a characterization seems overdrawn, however, based on the incidence of abuses reported in the field research.

Local Objectives and Skills Training

In 1976, Congress shifted the emphasis of PSE from creating jobs to meeting the needs of people with relatively few skills that were in demand in the job market.

A program such as PSE can benefit unskilled or low-skilled people in three ways. First, it can provide work experience—that is, training in the basic work skills and habits needed for any job, such as getting to work on time, plus the "credential" of successfully holding a job for an extended period. Second, PSE can provide on-the-job training in particular skills, such as typing or repairing trucks, that can lead to unsubsidized jobs later. Work experience alone does not provide this kind of specialized skills training. For on-the-job training to occur, however, two things must be true: the job must require some particular skills, and the participant must not possess that skill when he or she enters the program. If a program "creams" applicants by choosing only those who already have job skills, no training takes place. Such creaming was, in fact, occurring in PEP and in the early phases of PSE, as local government agencies sought to hire people who were already qualified. The 1976 restrictions on eligibility, then, were a way to expand the amount of on-the-job training that PSE was providing.

The third way a program such as PSE can benefit the unskilled is by providing formal training—that is, the kind of training usually conducted in a classroom, rather than on-the-job. Such training can either provide specific job-related skills or general skills, including such fundamental general skills as reading and mathematics. This type of training was not emphasized in PSE until the 1978 amendments, which required local governments to set aside certain percentages of PSE funds for formal training.

Whatever kind of training PSE was to provide, this goal was in conflict with the local objective of using PSE workers to produce additional public services. Training implies matching the job to the needs of the participant, while providing services requires matching the participant to the requirements of the job. The Brookings-Princeton field associates found that the latter was the practice during the early years of PSE in about three-quarters of the jurisdictions they observed. The shifts in emphasis required by the 1976 and 1978 amendments therefore necessitated changes in the characteristics of PSE participants and in the types of jobs they were assigned.

Changes in Participant Characteristics

Eligibility rules were quite loose for PEP and for PSE until 1976, a period that coincided with the heavy federal emphasis on job creation. Participants during this early period tended to be similar in many respects to most regular local government jobholders: predominantly male, white, and between the ages of 22 and 44.[2] Only three PEP participants out of eight were economically disadvantaged, and only one out of eight were receiving any form of public assistance at the time they enrolled. Characteristics of PSE participants during the first six months of 1975 were almost identical to those of PEP participants (see table 2-1).

Significant changes in participant characteristics became apparent in the first six months of 1977, when the tightened eligibility requirements for new Title VI enrollees had taken effect and the Carter administration's buildup of PSE enrollments was just beginning (column 3, table 2-1). Much larger percentages of new enrollees were economically disadvantaged, and twice as many as before had been receiving public assistance just before they joined the PSE program. These trends continued between October 1977 and September 1978 (fiscal year 1978). Sizable increases are found not only for the economically disadvantaged and welfare recipients, but also for those with less than a twelfth-grade education (columns 4 and 5). This movement to the more disadvantaged segment of the population was strongest in the projects portion of PSE (about half of new Title VI enrollees), but was also found in the sustainment portion (Title II enrollees and the rest of Title VI). As noted earlier, many program operators hired new participants for both portions of the program under the new rules for the project portion, so that PSE workers could be shifted between titles if needed.

The movement toward hiring the less advantaged accelerated after the 1978 eligibility restrictions took effect. The proportion of participants who were economically disadvantaged rose to 83 percent for those who joined the program between January and June 1979, and to 88 percent for those who joined between October 1979 and September 1980 (fiscal year 1980). Compared with figures for January-June 1977, the data for 1979 and 1980 also show larger proportions of women, blacks, and persons who did not go past eleventh grade. The percentages for Vietnam-era veterans and other veterans went down, partly because enrollments of women were going up.

According to the Brookings-Princeton field associates, persons enrolled in Title II-D (the new designation for the structural segment of the PSE program) were even more likely to be from disadvantaged portions of the population than were participants in Title VI, the countercyclical portion. As of December 1979, Title II-D figures were higher than Title VI for percentages of women (50 versus 45 percent), blacks (73 versus 67 percent), education of less than 12 years (29 versus 22 percent), and economically disadvantaged (96 versus 82 percent). Both titles showed significant changes from the past, but the emphasis on the disadvantaged was even stronger in Title II-D.

Table 2-1
Percent Distribution of New Enrollee Characteristics

Characteristic	PEP[a] (1)	PSE[b] Jan.-June 1975 (2)	PSE[c] Jan.-June 1977 (3)	PSE[d] Oct. 1977-Sept. 1978 Sustainment (4)	PSE[d] Oct. 1977-Sept. 1978 Project (5)	PSE[a] Jan.-June 1979 (6)	PSE[f] Oct. 1979-Sept. 1980 (7)
Sex							
Male	72	70	65	62	62	54	55
Female	28	30	35	38	38	46	45
Age							
Under 22	22	23	20	23	23	25	25
22-44	64	61	65	64	65	64	64
45 and over	14	16	15	13	12	11	12
Race							
White	64	65	66	65	58	56	51
Black	22	24	25	23	33	34	36
Other	14	12	9	12	9	10	12
Education (Grade)							
0-8	4[g]	10	8	8	11	8	9
9-11	22[g]	14	17	15	26	18	23
12	43	42	40	41	50	42	42
13+	31	34	35	36	14	32	26
Military							
Vietnam ERA veteran	27	19	16	16	12	11	8
Other veteran	14	12	13	10	19	10	10
Non-veteran	50	70	71	74	77	79	81

Economically disadvantaged	38	37	61	73	83[h]	83[h]	88[h]
Receiving public assistance	12	10	25	30	62	67	40

a. U.S. D.O.L. report as of November 30, 1972. Westat, Inc., *Longitudinal Evaluation of PEP and Validation of the PEP Data Bank: Final Report* (Washington, DC: U.S. Department of Labor, April 1975), Table 4-1.

b. New enrollees in PSE CLMS Followup Report No. 3, Table 1.

c. New enrollees in PSE CLMS Report No. 8, Fiscal Year 1977, Table 17.

d. U.S. Department of Labor CLMS Report No. 10, Characteristics of Enrollees Who Entered Adult Oriented CETA Programs During Fiscal Year 1978, Table 13.

e. Preliminary CLMS data, U.S. Department of Labor.

f. CLMS Report No. 14, Fiscal Year 1980, Table 8.

g. Grades 0-7 and grades 8-11.

h. Receiving cash welfare and/or below 70 percent of BLS lower living standard and/or below OMB poverty level income.

Changes in Types of Jobs
Held by Participants

The 1976 and 1978 amendments made it increasingly difficult for local governments to continue to "fit the worker to the job," as they did in PEP and early PSE. The shift toward more disadvantaged persons in these two sets of amendments, plus the introduction of a heavy emphasis on training as part of the 1978 amendments, made it necessary for governments to "fit the job to the worker."

This section presents data on changes in three aspects of public service job assignments:

- the types of services federally subsidized workers provided;

- the proportion of workers who were assigned to work in agencies of the government that operated the local program, compared with the proportion who were assigned to nonprofit community-based organizations or to agencies of governments other than the program operator; and

- the type of occupations workers held, such as clerical or paraprofessional.

Data are available on types of services provided by PEP workers, allowing us to make comparisons with data on PSE gathered in 1977, 1979, and 1980 by the Brookings-Princeton field associates. For the other two aspects of job assignments, however, we are able to make comparisons only between 1977 and later years, as no comparable information was gathered on PEP or the earlier years of PSE.

Types of Services

The general type of services provided by the largest proportions of public service job holders was "primary" services—that is, the kinds of services that all local governments provide and that are considered basic. Public service job holders were found, for example, in nonuniformed positions in police and fire departments (shown as "protective services" in table 2-2); in public works departments; in sanitation and related departments (shown as "environmental quality"); and in general administrative services such as personnel or payroll offices. (Note that the data for PEP do not include a general administration category; many of the workers shown in the miscellaneous category were probably employed in general administration jobs.) Smaller but still significant numbers of workers were assigned to governmental or nonprofit agencies providing social services; to parks and recreation agencies; and to school systems (shown as "education").

The following excerpts from the reports of associates indicate the variety of services that were provided.

In the early days of PSE the positions were deployed to stabilize primary services (i.e., public works, parks, real property) but the new project money is being used for more social services. Child care, drug treatment, and elderly care are representative of this branching out into variable services.

Some educational services would be cut back without PSE. In the school district we find teachers' aides and clerical workers in PSE slots. At the community college, PSE participants run special programs in drama, music, and vocational training. At the university, many PSE participants are research aides or clerical workers.

Brush clearing, park and recreation area improvement, record keeping, library services, and social services requiring extensive client contact have all been visibly improved by local PSE employment.

Two PSE projects have served as successful pilots which may lead to regional programs. One is a cancer screening and education program. Eleven other municipalities have shown an interest in sharing in this project. Some qualified personnel have been trained through this project.

Table 2-2
Types of Services Provided by PSE Enrollees

Characteristic	PEP[a] 1971-72	December 1977[b]		December 1979[b]	
		Sustainment	Project	II-D	VI
Primary services	41	58	45	25	42
Protective	17	19	1	6	11
Public works	19	11	16	9	19
Environmental quality	5	16	19	3	5
General administration	(3)	12	9	7	7
Social services	15	19	25	35	33
Social services	7	10	16	24	21
Health	8	6	7	7	7
Cultural	N.A.	3	2	4	5
Parks and recreation	9	17	15	5	8
Education	19	6	6	34	14
Miscellaneous	12	1	8	1	3
Total	100	100	100	100	100

a. Westat, Inc. *Longitudinal Evaluation of the Public Employment Program and Validation of the PEP Data Bank, Final Report*, U.S. Department of Labor, Office of Program Evaluation, Employment and Training Administration, Washington, DC, April 1975, Table 5.2.
b. Field evaluation data.

PSE has been a stimulus for the creation of many non-profit organizations in the county which now provide residents with a migrant health center, homemaker service, crisis intervention centers, and numerous other cultural and social service programs.

In considering the figures in table 2-3, it is useful to recall what restrictions were in effect at the periods shown on who could be hired for public service jobs. For PEP, restrictions were practically nonexistent; for the sustainment portion of PSE in 1977, some restrictions were in effect, but these were less stringent than those applying to the projects portion. As of 1979, hiring under Title II-D was more tightly restricted to the disadvantaged than under Title VI.

The effects of these restrictions are clear in some categories. In protective services, little difference can be seen between the percentage of workers assigned under PEP and those assigned in 1977 to the sustainment portion of PSE, but hardly any project workers were found in this category. By 1979, the proportions of both Title II-D and Title VI workers in this category were considerably smaller than the proportion under PEP, but the figure under the less restrictive Title VI was somewhat larger than under Title II-D. These shifts suggest that police and fire department officials did not consider the more disadvantaged workers hired under stringent eligibility rules to be as valuable as those hired under rules that allowed more qualified persons.

Aside from the protective services category, governments in 1977 employed substantial portions of PSE workers in the primary service areas of public works and environmental quality. The more disadvantaged participants in project positions were especially likely to be used in these areas, often as laborers on street repair and garbage disposal crews. This suggests that, despite the hiring restrictions in place as of 1977, local governments were able to use PSE workers for needed basic services.

Table 2-3
Percentage Distribution of PSE Participants by Title and Employing Agency
December 1977, 1979 and 1980

Title	Sample governments	Other local governments	School districts	Federal and state agencies	Nonprofit organizations
December 1977					
II and IV - sustainment......	65	6	14	4	10
VI - project.............	35	6	12	4	43
Overall average..........	52	6	13	4	25
December 1979					
II-D	34	11	22	2	31
VI	55	4	6	4	31
Overall average.........	44	7	15	3	31
December 1980					
II-D	33	11	22	3	31
VI	47	2	7	4	39
Overall average.........	39	8	16	3	34

SOURCE: Field study.

A countervailing trend had begun in 1977, however, and had gained strength by 1979. This was the increased tendency to assign PSE workers to nonprofit community-based organizations and to agencies of governments other than the prime sponsor. This trend will be discussed in the next section, but signs of it can be seen in table 2-3. One such sign is increases in percentages of workers performing social services, many of whom worked for nonprofit agencies. This category was espcially large in 1979. A second such sign is the sharp increase between 1977 and 1979 in the proportion of PSE workers assigned to school systems. By 1979, PSE workers were much less likely than before to be providing basic services for government agencies, and more likely to be providing social or educational services for agencies outside the local general-purpose government.

Use of PSE Workers by Nonprofit Agencies

Table 2-3 clearly shows the movement toward use of nonprofit organizations and agencies connected to governments outside the prime sponsor. In PEP, an estimated 10 percent of the workers had such assignments, most of them in school districts. In PSE as of December 1977, an overall average of 48 percent were working outside the local prime sponsor's own departments, a figure that increased to 56 percent in 1979 and 61 percent in 1980.

The use of workers in nonprofit organizations and agencies of outside governments was especially common in the portion of PSE that was more restricted to disadvantaged persons. In 1977, this was the projects portion; in the later years, it was Title II-D. In 1979 and 1980, the local governments in the Brookings-Princeton sample were retaining only about one-third of Title II-D workers for their own agencies. The percentage of Title VI workers retained by these governments was also falling, however, and this drop in Title VI accounts for the decline in overall retention figures between 1979 and 1980.

The decrease in the proportion of Title VI workers retained by local governments is all the more notable because the absolute number of Title VI workers was falling during this period in the jurisdictions covered by the Brookings-Princeton sample. Between 1979 and 1980, the total number of PSE workers in the sample dropped from 35,757 to 31,417, and the percentage accounted for by Title VI workers fell from 49 percent to 37 percent.

There was one conspicuous exception to this pattern. The large distressed cities in the sample adapted to the decline in the overall number of PSE positions by pulling back Title VI slots from nonprofit agencies and from agencies of outside governments (see table 2-4). As of December 1980, these distressed cities retained 80 percent of the Title VI positions for their own agencies and allocated only 12 percent to nonprofit organizations. By contrast, the pattern was almost reversed in cities that faced less fiscal pressure. These governments retained only 12 percent of their Title VI positions and subcontracted almost three-quarters to nonprofit organizations.

As the PSE program shrank nationwide, the distressed cities were trying to maintain services by pulling PSE positions back into their own agencies, or at least by cutting the number of slots in their own agencies less sharply than in other agencies. Less distressed cities and suburban and rural governments, by contrast, saw less value in the more restricted PSE and reduced the proportions of workers assigned to their own agencies.

Occupations and Wages

After the 1978 amendments took effect, local governments assigned PSE participants to lower-level jobs and paid lower average wages than before (see table 2-5). The percentage of workers in professional, technical, or managerial positions as of 1979 was about half of what it had been in 1977 and in

Table 2-4
Percentage Distribution of PSE Participants by Employing Agency and Title
December 1980

Type of jurisdiction and CETA title	Sample governments	Other local governments	School districts	Federal and state agencies	Nonprofit organizations	Total
Distressed large cities						
II-D	35	*	24	1	39	100
VI	80	*	8	*	12	100
Total	54	*	17	1	27	100
Other large cities						
II-D	34	19	23	*	24	100
VI	12	1	6	7	74	100
Total	26	13	17	3	40	100
Smaller cities and suburban areas						
II-D	25	12	13	17	34	100
VI	22	10	10	10	48	100
Total	24	11	12	15	38	100
Rural areas						
II-D	28	24	10	16	23	100
VI	34	22	11	11	22	100
Total	30	23	10	14	22	100

NOTE: Figures do not always add to 100 because of rounding.

*Less than 0.5 percent.

Table 2-5
Occupations and Average Wages of PSE Participants

Occupation	PEP[a]		December 1977[b]				December 1979[b]				December 1980[b]			
			Sustainment		Project		II-D		VI		II-D		VI	
	Percent	Wage	Percent	Wage	Percent	Wage	Percent	Wage	Percent	Wage	Percent	Wage	Percent	Wage
Prof., tech., mgr. ..	26	$3.34	28	$4.61	27	$4.39	14	$4.32	13	$4.71	15	$3.88	26	$4.29
Clerical..............	18	2.76	24	3.70	16	3.74	29	4.05	24	4.24	28	3.79	21	3.85
Craft................	2	2.98	3	4.85	4	4.33	2	5.01	3	6.23	2	3.62	6	3.90
Operative	1	2.98	6	4.46	3	4.13	2	5.71	3	6.36	5	4.02	2	4.35
Laborer.............	24	2.57	28	3.99	36	3.98	20	4.84	26	5.56	26	3.87	24	4.08
Service	22	2.72	12	4.18	13	3.77	33	4.35	30	5.04	20	3.93	19	3.78
Miscellaneous	7	2.81	--	--	--	--	--	--	--	--	5	3.85	1	3.23[c]
Total	100	2.87	100	4.50	100	4.24	100	4.32	100	5.10	100	3.85	100	4.02

NOTE: Percentages may not add to 100 because of rounding.

a. Sar A. Levitan and Robert Taggart, eds., *Emergency Employment Act: The PEP Generation* (Salt Lake City: Olympus, 1974), Table (I-6, I-2).

b. Field evaluation data.

c. Miscellaneous category for 1980 is composed of individuals who were full-time training and had only nominal jobs at the training site. 1980 figures are based on a stratified (by type of agency) random sample of 1,940 participants.

the PEP program, while the 1979 percentage for clerical workers was considerably higher than those for previous years. The proportion of positions classified as service jobs also increased between 1977 and 1979, although, as we saw earlier, the types of services provided were less likely to be protective services and more likely to be social services, such as day care.

The reasons for these shifts were clearly related to the changes in eligibility rules. The field associate in a distressed large city where half the new PSE participants had less than 12 years of education stated the following:

> Officials report that there is a difference in the characteristics of new PSE jobholders. The new group is less educated, averaging a fifth-grade education level. Many of the new PSE jobholders cannot read, necessitating an increased need to redefine PSE jobs as laborer, trainee, and helper positions.

As the PSE program began to shrink in size, the nature of the jobs underwent further changes. Between 1979 and 1980 the proportion of service jobs dropped sharply while increases occurred in labor and paraprofessional occupations. Taken together, clerical, labor, and service occupations accounted for about three-quarters of all Title II-D positions, and about two-thirds of all Title VI positions. In 1980, about 5 percent of Title II-D jobs and 1 percent of Title VI jobs were classified as "student," suggesting that some of those in training programs had no other job assignments.

Just as striking as the shift in occupations was the drop in average wage levels after 1978. Until that year, the law imposed a limit of $10,000 on the amount of federally subsidized wages any participant could be paid, but allowed local governments to supplement PSE workers' wages. The 1978 amendments ended governments' power to supplement wages, keeping the maximum at $10,000 though governments in high-wage areas were allowed to go up to $12,000.

The limitation on maximum wages had always been a major restriction on the kinds of jobs PSE workers could be assigned, because regulations also required local governments to pay PSE workers the same wages as regular employees at similar jobs. In many areas, regular municipal employees in many skilled occupations earned more than the PSE maximum. This meant that the restrictions on wages amounted to a restriction on the level of jobs PSE workers could hold and thus the types of services they could provide. From the federal perspective, these limits were necessary to prevent local governments from hiring skilled workers for PSE jobs, to direct positions to the disadvantaged, and to prevent inflationary pressure on wages in skilled occupations. The limits were also supported by unions of public employees, who feared that local governments might try to replace regular workers with subsidized PSE workers.

One way local governments stayed within the wage limits while technically complying with the rules requiring pay comparable to regular employees was to devise new personnel categories for PSE workers. As noted by the field associate quoted above, governments sometimes classified low-skilled, low-wage PSE workers as "aides," "trainees," or "helpers."

As the skill level of PSE enrollees declined, the use of such trainee positions increased and wages fell. Between 1979 and 1980, average wages fell by about 20 percent in Title VI and by more than 10 percent in Title II-D. Wages of Title VI participants in most occupations were higher than those for Title II-D workers in both years, but the gap was narrower in 1980.

At the time of the December 1980 field observation, average wages in Title VI in the sample governments were only 27 percent above the then-current minimum wage of $3.25 per hour, and those in Title II-D were only 19 percent above it. These data provide evidence that many local governments in 1979 were "segmenting" their PSE workers—that is, assigning the better qualified workers to

Title VI at higher wages than those earned by Title II-D workers in similar occupations. Evidence of this practice was less strong in 1980, though associates reported that it was still common in large distressed cities.

Summary

Public service job programs of the 1970s went through three stages. During the first stage, under PEP and the first three years of PSE, rules on eligibility were loose and local governments were able to hire just about anyone. This allowed the government agencies to readily meet their goals of providing services with the help of PSE workers. In the second stage, which began with the 1976 amendments, federal rules shifted to a greater emphasis on the disadvantaged, but local governments by and large were still able to meet their service provision objectives. During this period, the policy bargain we referred to at the beginning of this chapter was at work.

The third stage began with passage of the 1978 amendments imposing stringent limitations on the types of workers that local governments could hire under PSE. The size of the program was shrinking at the same time. With these changes, all except the most fiscally distressed localities reduced their use of PSE workers for basic services in government agencies. Large proportions of PSE workers were assigned to low-wage, low-skill occupations, many of them in nonprofit agencies. Provision of local government services was no longer one of the goals stated in the law; the policy bargain that had promoted local government cooperation was no longer in effect.

When the Reagan administration announced its intention to end PSE in 1981, many nonprofit agencies providing social services protested that they would have to severely cut back their operations without PSE workers. Local government officials, however, watched the end of PSE in relative silence; for them, its usefulness in helping provide public services was already past.

NOTES

1. Juan Cameron, "How CETA Became a Four-Letter Word." *Fortune* 99 (April 9, 1979): 112-114.

2. PSE characteristics data are, unless otherwise noted, from the Continuous Longitudinal Manpower Survey (CLMS), sponsored by the U.S. Department of Labor. Data on participants from a sample of about 140 prime sponsors were gathered by the U.S. Bureau of the Census and analyzed by Westat, Inc. of Rockville, MD.

3
The Job Creation
Impact of PSE

A primary measure of success for an employment and training program such as PSE is whether it creates more jobs than would have existed otherwise. PSE's success at job creation was always one of the major questions about the program, for reasons discussed in the previous chapter. Local government concerns with balancing budgets, providing adequate services, and limiting pressure on local tax capacities make for powerful incentives to take an outside resource such as PSE and direct it to these ends rather than to creating new jobs for the unemployed disadvantaged, as intended by the federal government.

Concern about conflicts in goals between the federal government and local governments influenced both the design and evaluation of the PSE program. Speculation concerning PSE and PEP suggested high rates of fiscal substitution and job displacement, and significant changes were made in the program's design, restricting local control over the program. The legislation under which these changes were enacted called for an evaluation of the job creation impact on PSE, and it was for this purpose that the public service employment field study was undertaken at the Brookings Institution and later at Princeton University. The results of that evaluation as they relate specifically to the job creation question are the subject of this chapter.

The chapter begins with a discussion of the concept of job creation and how it was operationalized in the Brookings-

Princeton field research. A detailed reporting of the results from four rounds of field observation is then presented. These observations span the period from July 1977 through December 1980, the period in which major revisions to the program's design were implemented, and encompass some forty jurisdictions.

The results of the field analysis indicate a consistently high rate of job creation, with between 80 and 90 cents of each PSE dollar contributing directly to job creation. As a further test of these findings, a statistical analysis was performed for a group of 30 large cities. The results of this analysis, based on annual financial data compiled by the U.S. Bureau of Census, are reported in an appendix to the chapter.

Defining and Measuring Job Creation

To assess the fiscal effects of any grant program, one must first reckon with the question of how these effects might manifest themselves. Simple notions of additivity and substitution described in grants theory take on subtle meanings within the actual fiscal environments of recipient governments.

In the case of PSE, the fundamental distinction is between job creation and job displacement. Did PSE have a direct effect in stimulating a higher level of employment than would otherwise have occurred and in what specific ways did such job creation manifest itself? There is the fairly straightforward pattern where local employment increases at a faster-than-normal rate. Yet, there are more subtle patterns where, in the absence of PSE, layoffs would have occurred due, perhaps, to weakening fiscal circumstances among recipient governments. Simple comparisons of pre- and post-PSE employment patterns are likely to miss such job creation effects.

Under job displacement, PSE-funded positions are substituted for those that would otherwise have been financed out of local revenue. This could arise as an accounting transaction, switching part of the current workforce on to a PSE-funded payroll, or as a more subtle pattern involving the addition of new, PSE-funded positions that were scheduled to be filled and financed out of local revenue. Underlying such displacement is the issue of fiscal substitution, a phenomenon inherent in all federal grant programs. It is through fiscal substitution that PSE is effectively transformed into a general revenue sharing program. Recipient governments are, as a result, less constrained in the use of PSE and the job creation impact is weakened.

The strength of any research design must ultimately be judged by how sensitive it is to the ways in which direct job creation manifests itself in local employment patterns, as well as to job displacement impacts arising from fiscal substitution uses of PSE.

Alternative Research Designs

Some researchers have attempted to gauge the effects of PSE according to the estimated impact of such assistance on total spending.[1] To the extent that PSE positions are subcontracted to nongovernmental agencies, such studies understate the total spending effect of PSE. Moreover, macro-level analyses of gross spending effects bring little or no refinement to bear on the nature of job creation and displacement impacts, nor do they provide any insight into variations in spending and employment effects across different segments of the state and local government sector.

Other researchers have used regression estimates of the total number of state and local jobs to see whether this total increased by an amount equal to the number of PSE positions. If the overall increase in state and local employment is less than the number of PSE jobs, they conclude that governments used federal funds for displacement.[2] By examining only aggregate state and local government employment, these researchers fail to account for the many PSE positions subcontracted to nonprofit organizations and the smaller number of slots subcontracted to federal agencies. This failure leads to an overestimate of displacement. At the same time, there is evidence that many governments used their own funds to add regular employees to administer the PSE program and supervise PSE workers. To the extent this occurs, examination of aggregate employment may result in estimates of displacement that are too low.

A third group of researchers has tried to estimate the trend in local government employment and relate any deviation from this trend to the number of PSE positions. This approach tends to overestimate displacement for two reasons. First, like the two methods just mentioned, it fails to account for subcontracting to nongovernmental employing agencies. Second, it fails to consider the possibility that the rate of growth in local government employment has slowed because of citizen concern over mounting expenditures and property taxes.[3]

The Brookings-Princeton Framework

The Brookings-Princeton field associates used the following framework in determining whether a particular use of a PSE worker constituted job creation or displacement:

Job Creation

- *New programs and services:* Cases in which additional programs or services were provided with PSE funding that would not otherwise have been undertaken.

- *Special projects:* New, one-time projects lasting one year or less that were undertaken with PSE funds.

- *Program expansion:* Cases in which the level of services was raised or services were improved under existing programs by using PSE funds beyond what they would be with local funds.

- *Program maintenance:* Cases in which PSE employees were used to maintain existing services that would have been curtailed without PSE funding. This is considered job creation because total employment was higher than it otherwise would have been.

Job Displacement

- *Transfers:* Cases involving the transfer of existing state and local government positions to PSE funding.

- *Rehires:* Cases in which state or local employees were laid off and then rehired with PSE funding.

- *Contract reduction:* Cases in which PSE participants were used to provide services or to work on projects that had been, or normally would have been, contracted to an outside organization or private firm.

- *Potential hires:* Cases in which PSE participants were hired to fill positions that otherwise would have been funded with other revenue.

Using this framework, the job creation category captures instances where PSE funds were unaffected by fiscal substitution, resulting in the direct creation of jobs and a higher level of employment than would have existed in the absence of PSE. Under job displacement, on the other hand, the employment impact is confounded by fiscal substitution. In the case of "transfers," for example, PSE-funded workers displace previously employed workers, creating a possible effect on the composition of local employment, but undermining the program's direct impact on the level of employment, subsequent uses of freed-up local revenue notwithstanding.[4] In the case of "rehires," fiscal substitution undermines the impact of PSE on both the level and composition of local employment patterns. From this categorization, it follows that while displacement uses of PSE do not preclude compositional effects on local employment patterns or longer term effects on employment levels, the overall strength and timing of such effects are much more uncertain.

Program Maintenance

The program maintenance category turned out to be of considerable importance in accounting for the job creation impact of PSE, particularly among larger, fiscally distressed cities. In effect, the associates determined that these cities would have cut certain services, but instead were able to keep them going with PSE funds.

Such uses are not considered to be displacement because the positions in question would not have been funded without the PSE program. The essential question is whether attitudes toward local public services had shifted in the mid-seventies enough to cause some jurisdictions to cut services or expand them more slowly at the time the PSE program was expanding. To the extent that the level of local government employment departed in this way from its historic upward trend, an econometric or simple trend study would overstate the displacement effects of PSE because it would overpredict aggregate state and local employment.[5]

Other researchers have noted that growth in local public employment had begun to slow even before California voters passed Proposition 13 in 1977, a referendum that required state and local governments to roll back property tax rates and imposed restrictions on their ability to raise rates in the future. For example, George Peterson of the Urban Institute testified in July 1978: "For the quarter century ending in 1975, local public spending rose year in and year out relative to national product, but, during the present economic recovery, city expenditures have grown at a much slower rate than national output. Cities suffering economic and population declines have taken the lead in restraining expenditures."[6]

A similar pattern was observed for the large cities in the study, actually beginning prior to 1975. The 16 cities are divided in table 3-1 into two groups—large distressed cities and other large cities.[7] The table shows the change in full-time-equivalent noneducational employment in the distressed and other large cities as well as in cities as a whole. These figures from the U.S. Bureau of the Census include PSE workers retained by the city for positions in their own agencies. Also shown in table 3-1 are the estimated population change from 1970 through 1976 and the number of PSE participants in December 1977 as a percentage of the total number of city government employees in 1976.

Table 3-1
Selected Data on Employment Trends
in the Brookings-Princeton Sample Cities
1970-1976

City	Percentage change in total noneducational employment 1970-1976[a]	Percentage change in population 1970-1976[b]	PSE employees in the city government December 1977 as a percentage of 1976 employment[c]
Large distressed cities			
Baltimore	−13[d]	−9	10
Boston	−4	−6	11
Cleveland	−36	−17	14
Detroit	−23	−13	14
New Orleans	+8	−2	10
Philadelphia	+8	−8	11
Rochester	−27	−11	11
St. Louis	0	−17	13
Total	−9	−10	12
Other large cities			
Chicago	+10	−9	8
Houston	+51	+15	9
Kansas City	+15	−10	16
Los Angeles	+5	−2	9
Phoenix	+42	+14	16
San Francisco	+6	−7	12
St. Paul	+19	−12	8
Tulsa	+28	+1	11
Total	+13	−2	10
All cities	+12		

a. From U.S. Census Bureau, *City Employment, 1966-1976*. Includes PSE positions.

b. From Department of the Treasury, Office of Revenue Sharing, *Initial State and Local Data Elements, Enrollment Period 10*.

c. From Brookings field data. Excludes all subcontracted and outstationed positions.

d. Data for 1976 include employment in municipally operated institutions of higher education.

For all cities combined, city noneducational employment increased by 12 percent in this period. Among the other large cities in the Brookings-Princeton sample (the second group in table 3-1), total employment increased by 13 percent, even though the population of these jurisdictions declined by 2 percent. PSE employees amounted to roughly 10 percent of the workers in these city governments.

In sharp contrast, total city employment (including PSE employment) in the distressed large cities in the sample decreased by 9 percent between 1970 and 1976. The declines for Cleveland, Detroit, and Rochester were 36, 23, and 27 percent, respectively. Since 1972, the peak year for employment in this group of cities, employment levels in all of them have declined.

As a group, distressed large cities were aided disproportionately under the PSE program. The distressed large cities in the sample accounted for 4 percent of all PSE enrollees as of December 1977, but only 1 percent of total state and local employment. This concentration of PSE positions in the governments that appear in other respects to be departing from the trend line of city employment adds to the difficulty of conducting econometric or trend-type studies of the program's employment impact.

This finding of local employment cutbacks in some of the sample jurisdictions applied not only to large cities but to small ones as well. Following is a quote from the field research associate for a small city in the sample indicating much the same shift. The associate concludes that the onset of "a period of fiscal austerity" has hardened attitudes against the use of PSE positions for displacement purposes.

> By 1976, the climate had changed dramatically. Most of the major projects the city council members wanted to achieve had been completed. Taxes had increased substantially and the city was

beginning to experience its first real pressure from the suburbanization of business. The 1976 council election revolved around the issue of taxes. Conservatives won two of the three seats up for election. The remaining three members had sensed the attitude of the voters before the 1976 election and the election outcome confirmed their interpretation. A period of fiscal austerity ensued, presided over by the same city manager who had been an expansionist in earlier years. As the next election draws near, economic development and stable taxes are the main concerns of the elected officials. The city manager's policy toward PSE has been consistent with the council's stated intention of not raising taxes. Thus the political-administrative climate is against converting PSE positions to unsubsidized positions.

A field associate's appraisal of local fiscal conditions and prospects determined whether the associate considered a government's use of PSE workers to be program maintenance. If the associate determined on the basis of interviews and financial and employment data that the fiscal pressure (real or perceived) on a jurisdiction was so severe as of the observation date that the jurisdiction would have cut existing service levels, then using PSE employees to maintain these services was classified as program maintenance and was not at that time regarded as displacement. Alternatively, if the associate determined that a jurisdiction had used PSE funds to maintain services that in his or her judgment would have been provided with other revenue, this was a case of displacement of the potential-hire variety.

Field Research Findings on Job Creation

Information bearing on the job creation impact of PSE was collected over four rounds of field observations. The first observation was made in July 1977, just after Congress had required half of Title VI participants to be employed in projects and had tightened eligibility requirements. Between the first observation and the second, in December 1977, the size of the program had doubled; as a result, many of the positions that were involved in the analysis of net employment effects were newly created. As part of the 1977 buildup, prime sponsors (local governments designated as direct recipients of PSE grants) were also encouraged to place an increasing share of PSE workers with nonprofit agencies through subcontracting arrangements. From the second round to the third round of observations in December 1979, the total size of the program was reduced by nearly half, the eligibility requirements were significantly tightened, and Congress reduced the wages that could be paid as well as a local government's ability to supplement wages with local revenue. A tenure limit was also imposed on participants. The final round of field observations occurred in December 1980, by which time the earlier program amendments governing wage rates and tenure had been fully implemented.

Table 3-2 summarizes the information on job creation and displacement uses of PSE for each of the four rounds of field observations.[8] Looking over the field data, a consistent pattern emerges indicating a very high proportion of PSE funds used for job creation. Most of the job creation activity is accounted for through expansions of existing services and program maintenance uses of PSE.

Although a more detailed breakout of the field data is necessary to understand the particular circumstances that shaped local responses to PSE, the very high rate and consistent pattern of job creation is noteworthy, particularly in view of earlier studies reporting a much greater tendency toward displacement. As noted above, conventional grants theory points up the possibility of conflicting goals between grantor and grantee which, in the case of PSE, might limit the program's job creation impact. However, the field research found that the tendency for local governments to use federal funds for fiscal relief was limited by three important factors.

Table 3-2
Job Creation and Displacement Rates
for All PSE Positions Sampled in Each Round
of the Brookings-Princeton Field Study

	July 1977	December 1977	December 1979	December 1980
Job creation	82	85	85	89
New services	9	14	12	
Expansion of existing services .	31	44	31	N.A.
Special projects ...	12	13	7	
Program maintenance	31	15	35	
Job displacement	18	15	14	11
Transfers	7	3		
Rehires	*	*	N.A.	N.A.
Potential hires	8	10		
Contract reduction	1	1		
Other	2	*		
Total	100	100	100	100

First, laws and regulations administered by the Department of Labor prohibited the use of PSE grant funds for fiscal relief. In this respect, PSE differed from general revenue sharing.

Second, local officials considered the PSE program to be temporary and its future funding uncertain and, therefore, did not want to rely on PSE for fiscal relief, unless it was absolutely necessary to do so. Because PSE was an operating grant rather than a capital grant, a local government that used these funds to provide ongoing services or continuing fiscal relief could have found itself forced to boost taxes if federal funding was discontinued or significantly reduced. Clearly the history of PSE and its predecessor raised doubts about the continuity of this federal funding.

Finally, local officials were in sympathy with the federal objectives; that is, they shared the federal objectives of reducing unemployment and providing additional jobs for the disadvantaged. The field associates found that, in some places, "generalist" local officials—such as the mayor and budget director, who were responsible for the entire city—were more likely to place a high value on uses of PSE for fiscal relief, while directors of employment and training offices or departments, who implemented PSE, were more likely to agree with the employment and training objectives of PSE. Even generalist officials by and large recognized the value of training and job creation, however.

Legal restrictions and attitudes toward uncertainty notwithstanding, it might be argued that displacement uses of PSE would be expected to increase over time. But to make a general statement that displacement would increase over time, one must assume that the size and character of the program would remain stable. In a stable program, displacement might increase as jurisdictions adjusted each new year's budget to take account of PSE positions. In fact, however, the PSE program was anything but stable. Its size, regulations, and level of funding all shifted almost constantly over the four rounds of field observations.

The doubling in the size of the program between the first and second rounds, together with the implementation of tighter eligibility criteria and restrictions on the types of jobs to which PSE participants could be assigned, would be expected to enhance the job creation impact of PSE. When Congress suddenly adds large amounts of money to a grant program, local governments cannot instantly substitute the added federal money for locally-raised revenue, because program and hiring decisions are made well in advance and cannot usually be reversed at the drop of a bundle of federal dollars. Similarly, tighter restrictions on the types of persons eligible to be hired with the PSE funds and on the types of jobs to which they may be assigned make it more difficult to substitute PSE-funded workers for those who would otherwise be funded out of local revenue sources.

Other forces that held displacement down included the provisions in the 1978 CETA amendments which extended tighter eligibility criteria to PSE workers funded under Title II-D. The 1978 amendments also restricted wage levels and supplementation of participant wages and thus the ability of governments to place workers in high-paying jobs, and limited a PSE worker's tenure in the subsidized job to eighteen months. These amendments made PSE workers less attractive for use in the kinds of jobs ordinarily filled by regular government employees, and so reduced the temptation to use PSE for displacement. Because of the new restrictions and the training requirements, many governments subcontracted larger proportions of their PSE workers to nonprofit organizations, which, as discussed later, were less likely to use them for displacement.

The restriction on tenure forced many local governments to either fire many PSE workers or absorb them into regular permanent jobs when they reached the limit on October 1, 1979, just three months before the third round of field observations. Presumably, a substantial number of those who might have been filling positions that constituted displacement were out of the PSE program by the December 1979 observation.

Without the change in the legislation, displacement would almost certainly have increased in the third round of field observations. Probably most important are the wage, supplementation, and tenure limits. Because of the decline in the size of the program, local governments would have pulled back to those positions in the government that were considered most essential. However, as noted earlier, the tenure limit led to the absorption of large numbers of PSE workers into the regular payroll on October 1, 1979, and many of these absorbed positions had previously been identified as displacement. Further, despite the large reduction in the program, the share of positions retained by the governments declined, due largely to the wage limits and the training requirements in the new legislation.

Some of these points were illustrated by the reports of the associates. An associate in a suburban county reported:

> Displacement is not as prevalent as it was in the first and second rounds. The major reason for this is that most of the agencies and local governments that were using the program for regular employment have dropped out of PSE. Many school districts and small local governments in the outlying areas of the county have chosen not to continue their affiliation with PSE. The reasons cited were that:
>
> 1. The wages were so low that they cannot create jobs in protective services, utilities, and sanitation, areas where they could use more employment.
>
> 2. The changes in personnel requirements that would allow continued use of PSE are resisted by the existing regular workers.
>
> 3. The people who are eligible for the program are unsuited for the jobs the government can or would want to create.

As the impact of the 1978 amendments filtered through the program, a number of agencies absorbed their current PSE slots and made it clear that they were disappointed with the program. In brief, they stated that there was no longer anything in PSE for them. From the associate in a distressed large city:

> The wage limits and the new eligibility rules have severely limited the ability of the local government to use CETA funds to hire more skilled employees in administrative and technical positions. Without these restrictions, the city would use more of the CETA money for higher paid employees who would perform normal city functions.

Variations in Net Employment Effects

Job creation and displacement rates varied in several ways—by type of employing agency, between the two titles of the act, from one type of jurisdiction to another, and among jurisdictions facing varying levels of fiscal pressure. The following sections analyze these variations.

By Type of Employing Agency

As part of the 1977 expansion of PSE, prime sponsors were encouraged to use nonprofit agencies in placing PSE workers. Such placements to nonprofit agencies, as well as to school districts, other local governments, and state and federal agencies, involved two kinds of arrangements: subcontracting and outstationing. Outstationing refers to employees who are paid by a prime sponsor government and carried as employees of that government, but in fact work for some other entity or agency. Generally, this was done as an administrative arrangement that allowed smaller organizations that did not have developed payroll systems to employ PSE employees, but have their wages paid by the prime sponsor government. In other cases, particularly in the smaller jurisdictions, it was done as a matter of administrative convenience.

Subcontracting was far more common than outstationing. Under the subcontracting arrangements, PSE participants were employees of the subcontracting agency, which was reimbursed on a contractual basis by the prime sponsor government.

An increasing share of PSE workers were employed through subcontracting arrangements (mainly with non-profit organizations) over the period from December 1977 through December 1980 (see table 2-3). In addition, there was a pronounced shift in the type of PSE-funded worker retained by the sample governments operating as prime sponsors. While nearly two-thirds of the Title II and Title VI sustainment slots were retained by these governments as of December 1977, Title VI project slots became the preferred use of PSE workers in 1979 and 1980. This largely reflects rule changes governing eligibility, training, and local supplementation of wages, the net effect of which made Title II-D assistance more restrictive.

Information on uses of PSE by type of employing agency is provided in table 3-3. These data are as of the third round of field observations. Except for some upward drift in program maintenance over four rounds of field observations, the patterns of net employment effects reported as of December 1979 are consistent with those observed in the other rounds.

High rates of job creation noted earlier were found in each type of employing agency, ranging from a low of 80 percent for the sample governments to a high of 93 percent for non-profit organizations. Among the job creation categories, program maintenance accounted for roughly half of the positions retained by the sample governments and of those subcontracted to school districts.

Table 3-3
Percentage Distribution of Employment Effects by Employing Agency
December 1979

Effect	Sample governments	Other local governments	School districts	Federal and state agencies	Nonprofit organizations
Job creation	80	87	86	90	93
New programs and services	6	1	8	10	26
Expansion of existing programs	21	70	22	60	39
Special projects	5	8	1	15	12
Program maintenance	48	8	54	5	16
Job displacement	20	13	14	10	7
Total	100	100	100	100	100

NOTE: Totals may not add due to rounding.

Commenting on such uses, the associate in a large, fiscally distressed city noted:

> Almost all of the city's sample positions were classified as job creation due to the severe financial conditions of the city. Seventy-one percent of all city positions were classified as program maintenance—usually because the employment trend analysis indicated that PSE had enabled the city to maintain a "traditional" level of service. This was especially true in Title VI where almost everyone is program maintenance. These positions included waste collectors, municipal laborers, and major portions of the recreation department. Title II-D had more service expansion than Title VI. Most expansion was in low-skill jobs (municipal service laborers, junior clerks, and truck drivers) and usually occurred when many PSE workers were hired in one category—at least a portion of which were classified as program maintenance.

In local governmental agencies outside the prime sponsor governments and in state and federal agencies, most positions were used to expand existing programs. Schools used many PSE workers for program maintenance, but also expanded programs by using PSE workers as teacher aides, hall monitors, and lunchroom workers or as counselors or medical screeners. Local government agencies outside the sample governments often used PSE workers as deputies in the sheriff's department, as librarian assistants, and in similar jobs that expanded the operations of the government beyond what would be funded out of local revenue.

In state and federal agencies, the expansion of existing programs meant more hours of service in an office, expansion of social services to additional areas or more clients, more workers in the state parks, equipment that was better maintained, and the like.

Nonprofit organizations were the only agencies providing significant levels of new services with PSE. Expansion of existing services and new programs accounted for virtually all of the job creation within nonprofit organizations. An example from a large city:

> Local services provided as a result of job creation outside City Hall included an artist-in-residence program reaching youth, aged, handicapped, and minority audiences; day care; clerical and bilingual assistance for area teachers; custodial and maintenance assistance for area schools and community-based organizations; and education, nutrition, recreation, and transportation services to the city's dependent populations (senior citizens, youth, minorities, handicapped, disadvantaged).

Displacement uses of PSE were primarily identified with the "potential hire" category, and were somewhat higher among the prime sponsor or program agent governments in the sample. Over time, displacement often occurred in services that came to have lives of their own. For example, recreation programs and such social service programs as transportation for the elderly and "meals on wheels" developed constituents who would demand that they be supported out of other sources in the absence of PSE. In other cases of displacement, nonprofit organizations used PSE funds in place of privately raised revenue, salting away the savings toward the day when PSE was no longer available. Such uses were identified by an associate in a distressed large city:

> Displacement in nonprofit organizations with Title II-D training projects is very low since many of the PSE participants do not provide essential services but rather are receiving training. Many nonprofit agencies are having their first experience with PSE employees and have not yet put them in critical job slots. However, some nonprofit agencies have hired

PSE participants to operate fork lifts, drive buses, and perform other tasks for which the employee can become essential. In these cases, the agencies have indicated that without PSE funding, they would probably be able to find other money to keep these employees on the job.

Variation by Title

As noted earlier, Title VI became the preferred title by the sample jurisdictions because of rule changes related to eligibility, training and local supplementation of wages. In the second round, the sample governments retained a higher proportion of Title II and Title VI sustainment positions than of the Title VI project positions, but by the third round they retained more Title VI positions and subcontracted more Title II-D positions.

Table 3-4 shows that this preference for Title VI was reflected in both the extent of displacement and in the degree of program maintenance. Displacement was somewhat

Table 3-4
Percentage Distribution of Net Employment Effects by Title
December 1979

Effect	Title II-D	Title VI
Job creation	87	84
New programs and services	17	8
Expansion of existing services	37	25
Special projects	4	9
Program maintenance	29	42
Job displacement	13	16
Total	100	100

higher and program maintenance accounted for a much greater share of job creation uses under Title VI, a pattern consistent with that observed earlier for the prime sponsor governments. Correspondingly, smaller proportions of Title VI participants were used to provide new programs and services or to expand existing services than was the case with Title II-D participants. Again, this pattern is consistent with the uses made of the PSE program by the prime sponsor governments compared with the uses made by nonprofit organizations and other employing agencies.

Variation by Type of Sample Government

As might be expected, large cities facing severe fiscal distress were the most likely to use PSE workers to maintain programs that otherwise would have been cut back or eliminated (see table 3-5). Most of these cities have declining populations, declining tax bases, and fairly high demands for public services. About one-fifth of the PSE positions in these jurisdictions were judged to represent displacement, with PSE workers assigned to basic services that the associate judged would have had to be maintained out of local revenue in the absence of PSE funding.

In the other large cities that faced less fiscal distress, prime sponsor governments subcontracted substantial numbers of PSE workers to outside agencies. These cities had nearly twice the proportion of workers who were providing for expansions of existing service levels. However, a fairly high proportion (34 percent) of the positions in these jurisdictions were classified as program maintenance and only 10 percent were categorized as displacement.

Smaller cities and suburban areas had more than half of all their PSE positions involved in expanding service levels or special projects.

Rural Areas

Rural areas and governments served by balance of state prime sponsors[9] stand out from other types of governments in two ways. First, they showed the highest levels of displacement. Second, when they used PSE to create jobs, they were

Table 3-5
Percentage Distribution of Net Employment Effects by Type of Jurisdiction December 1979

Effect	Large distressed cities	Other large cities	Small cities and suburban counties	Rural and balance of state areas
Job creation	82	90	84	69
New programs and services	13	11	15	10
Expansion of existing services . . .	22	38	32	41
Special projects	4	6	20	10
Program maintenance	42	34	16	8
Job displacement	18	10	16	31
Total	100	100	100	100
Addendum: Number of jobs	14,949	17,052	3,021	1,149

NOTE: Totals may not add due to rounding.

more likely than other governments to do so by expanding existing services.

Two reasons account for these findings. First, in many of these areas the primary users of PSE were local governments and school districts; very few nonprofit organizations were available to employ PSE workers. Second, the governments themselves perform more limited functions than governments in large cities, so that PSE participants were more likely to be employed in basic service areas.

A major use of PSE participants in these areas involved the provision of deputies for small towns and county sheriffs' offices. For example, a town may have had a single police officer. Often for the price of sending a person to police cadet school, the sheriff could have a force of deputies funded out of PSE. The citizens had more police protection and the town council was happy. When they finished their PSE jobs, the individual participants were often hired directly by the town or county in their existing jobs. PSE participants were also used in these areas as jailers or matrons in the county jail or as workers on the county road crews—both primary and important functions of small rural governments. In many of these situations, the use of the PSE worker constituted displacement.

The other prevalent kind of employment in rural areas was in clerical positions, such as clerks in the state police barracks and the county courthouse or dispatchers in the sheriff's office. Depending on the circumstances, the associate would classify these uses as either expansions of existing functions or, if the positions would otherwise have been funded out of local revenue, displacement.

The following reports from associates in two rural counties typify the kind of classification decision that had to be made:

> I put the county ambulance service in the displacement category. The state now mandates that the

ambulance service exist and thus the county has no real choice. I believe that they would have found the money even though it would have been difficult; however, the CETA program clearly made it easier for them to comply with the state mandate. In the most prosperous county, I have also put three deputy sheriffs under displacement since the county has now become very dependent on them and could probably afford to hire them.

*   *   *

The activities classified as displacement are highly diverse. To start with some of the more obvious, the county has acquired a mechanic and a mechanic's assistant to maintain county vehicles. This would otherwise be contracted out. Two townships are using PSE slots for assessor aides to help with two reassessments mandated by law. Without the PSE people, this would probably have to be hired out. The county is using a PSE person as liaison with the state police and has an additional three PSE slots in the county sheriff's office. I judged all of these to be potential hires because they are long term positions and staff additions have been made around the PSE slots.

Variation by Degree of Fiscal Pressure

Over the four rounds of field observations, the degree of fiscal pressure proved to be an important determinant of both the proportion of PSE slots retained by the sample governments and the net employment effects of the program. Associates were asked to judge the degree of fiscal pressure faced by the sample governments according to the following categories:

Extreme Fiscal Pressure: Previous service levels had been cut back to essential services. Own-source local revenue and anticipated external sources of revenue were insufficient to meet the demands for those services and there was no apparent source of increases in locally raised revenue in the coming year or so.

Moderate Fiscal Pressure: Anticipated own-source local revenue and external sources were expected to be insufficient to support the existing level of services. Maintaining the level of services in the jurisdiction would require a difficult positive action such as a new tax source, a significant increase in tax rates, or cuts in service levels.

Little Fiscal Pressure: Anticipated internal and external revenue (using existing sources with possible small rate increases) are expected to cover anticipated expenditures increases and service demands.

No Fiscal Pressure: The jurisdiction was experiencing increases in existing surpluses or had made voluntary tax cuts. There was no difficulty in meeting expected demands for essential services with existing internal and external revenue sources and tax rates.

In explaining how they classified a jurisdiction, associates provided both objective data and narrative statements. The former included data on the trend of year-end cash balances, the rate of growth of taxes and expenditures, the presence or absence of fund deficits, the use of short-term borrowing, increases or decreases in the tax base, the current bond rating, and increases or decreases in tax rates. The latter category included assessments by local officials of the capacity of the jurisdiction to expand activities or add new programs or services and the legal or political feasibility of a tax increase. The following excerpts from associate reports indicate the varying degrees of fiscal pressure in three of the sample cities.

From a large distressed city:

The city finds itself under extreme fiscal pressure. Several factors contribute to this conclusion, leaving little doubt to the validity of this assessment. Significant to this discussion are the following:

1. Increasing dependence on nonlocally raised revenues.

2. A shrinking population, resulting in a shrinking tax base and an increasingly dependent population.

3. Continued and increasing layoffs of city employees.

4. Reduced ability to borrow because of the bond ratings.

5. Negative local assessment of the city's ability to raise more tax revenues; the city's tax rate is four times the state average.

6. A predicted budget shortfall.

From a large city under moderate fiscal pressure:

Uncertainty about the city's fiscal health led Standard and Poors to downgrade the city's long-term bonds from AA to A-plus. The mayor's response in the 1980 budget was an unusually stringent fiscal program: only a 1 percent increase in the total budget; a personnel cutback of about 1,500 positions; a bundle of increased fees, charges, and taxes expected to yield about $100 million in new revenues; plus an $82 million increase in the 1979 tax levy—the first such increase since the early 1970s. This was the nastiest medicine any mayor had spooned out for a long time, but the general reaction was that higher taxes had to be swallowed in order to avoid New York- or Cleveland-style fiscal pneumonia.

From a large city with little fiscal pressure:

This rating was given for the following reasons:

1. A triple-A bond rating by both Standard and Poors and Moody.

2. Continued cash surpluses.

3. A stable nominal tax rate.

4. A stable assessment ratio.

5. Continued expansion of the tax base.

6. Low debt ratios.

7. A decrease in the expenditure growth rate.

8. A relatively low level of economic dependence on external funds.

9. Conservative fiscal and budgetary policies.

As of the third round of field observations in 1979, just under half of the governments in the sample were characterized as under relatively little or no fiscal pressure, 35 percent under moderate pressure, and 17 percent under extreme pressure. Reflecting the deterioration in the national economy, fiscal conditions worsened in 19 of the sample governments between the 1979 and 1980 observations, with 30 percent characterized as under relatively light or no fiscal pressure, 40 percent under moderate pressure, and 22 percent under extreme pressure in 1980.

As expected, the portion of PSE slots retained by the sample governments (as opposed to subcontracting with nonprofit organizations and other local governments) varied directly with fiscal pressure. By round four of the field observations, the sample governments under extreme fiscal pressure retained just over half of the PSE slots, compared to 43 percent and 39 percent for the governments under moderate and relatively light or no fiscal pressure, respectively.

Information on net employment effects by degree of fiscal pressure is presented in table 3-6. Not surprisingly, the jurisdictions facing extreme fiscal pressure had the highest proportions of positions devoted to maintaining and expanding existing services and had relatively little displacement. No positions in any of these jurisdictions were judged to be assigned to special projects.

Table 3-6
Percentage Distribution of Net Employment Effects
Within Sample Governments Only
by Degree of Fiscal Pressure
December 1979

	Degree of fiscal pressure		
Effect	Extreme	Moderate	Little or none
Job creation	94	69	82
New programs or services ..	7	3	12
Expansion of existing services	30	13	27
Special projects	1	3	30
Program maintenance	56	50	13
Job displacement	6	31	18
Total	100	100	100

Jurisdictions with little or no fiscal pressure had the highest proportions of special projects and had relatively little program maintenance. The largest proportion of the positions was used to provide new services or to expand existing services.

Jurisdictions with moderate fiscal pressure had the highest proportion of displacement (almost one-third of the positions). Four-fifths of the PSE positions retained by the sample government in these jurisdictions were in the category of program maintenance or displacement. It should be remembered that the definition of moderate fiscal pressure was that existing local revenue would soon be insufficient to support existing service levels, requiring either a tax increase or a cut in services. Obviously, to those possibilities must be added the use of federal PSE funds to fill the gap and provide fiscal relief.

The Fiscal Effects of PSE

As noted at the beginning of this chapter, the job creation effect and the fiscal impact of the PSE program are somewhat different issues. Displacement may reduce the amount of direct job creation, but whether or not there is a fiscal stimulus depends upon how the jurisdiction uses the funds freed up through displacement. If the released funds are used to expand services elsewhere in the government, the fiscal effect would still be one of higher expenditures in the public sector, even if there is less direct job creation than desired. Alternatively, if the released funds are used to reduce or stabilize taxes, there would still be a stimulus effect, but its initial impact would be in the private sector; the nature and magnitude of the effect would be similar to that of a federal tax cut.

While the primary concern of the field evaluation study was with the direct employment effects of PSE in the public sector, an attempt was made to determine, to the extent possible, how jurisdictions used the funds released by displacement.

Local revenue freed by displacement uses of PSE can be used in one of three basic ways:

1. Avoiding an increase in local taxes—that is, tax stabilization.

2. Spending the freed local money on other employment or capital projects.

3. Allowing the money to accumulate as idle fund balances.

The first of these alternatives allows the unused local money to stay in the pockets of taxpayers while maintaining government spending. The second lets the government increase discretionary spending. Only the third alternative has no immediate stimulative impact on either the private or public sectors.

As of the third round of field observations, 14 percent of all the PSE slots encompassed by the field research and 20 percent of the slots retained by the sample governments were identified as displacement uses of PSE. Of the money saved by the sample governments through displacement, the field associates estimated that approximately 40 percent was accounted for by tax stabilization. Almost one-fourth of the money was used to increase local spending in other ways (mostly for locally funded government employment), and the same proportion was set aside in fund balances. About one-eighth (12 percent) could not be allocated to any of these fiscal effects.

The use of local funds freed by displacement for tax stabilization is understandable. Local officials are reluctant to raise taxes even when costs rise; if PSE can fill the gap, there is a motivation for displacement. A number of reports indicate this sort of position. From a suburban county:

> For the most part, displacement by local government has had a tax stabilizing effect. The fiscal effects of increasing population growth have not totally offset the costs of increased service delivery demands, especially in the smaller municipalities. Displaced positions primarily represent essential protective services. PSE and increased county capabilities have "temporarily" delayed the inevitable—a millage increase.

As noted earlier, the situation in rural areas was somewhat different from that of the cities. Some of the displacement in these areas was the result of mandated services that had no revenue sources associated with them. The following is an example from a rural county:

> I put all the ambulance service employees under "tax stabilization" since I have reasoned that if

they are displacement then the money would have to come from somewhere if CETA did not exist and the only place it could come from is a tax increase for the support of the ambulance services. Indeed, this is one of the few categories where a tax increase would even be legal since the county is already at the legal limit in most other taxing categories. Since the program is mandated by the state, I suppose a tax increase to support this service would have been necessary.

Although tax reduction (as distinguished from the avoidance of a tax increase) was not very prevalent, one place it occurred was a smaller city where the associate reasoned as follows:

The conclusion that these funds represent tax reduction is based on: (1) declining municipal tax rates; (2) the mayor's public commitment to lowering tax rates; (3) the ability to finance desired expenditures through a growing tax base; and (4) an explicit statement by a local official that CETA money has reduced the sewer tax rate.

Summary of Field Research Findings

Viewed over the four rounds of field observations between July 1977 and December 1980, the impact of PSE can be summarized as follows:

1. Overall, displacement uses of PSE remained consistently low, ranging from 18 percent as of July 1977 to 11 percent as of December 1980. Among the factors contributing to the low displacement rate were changes in legislation affecting wage supplementation, tenure limits, and tighter eligibility criteria. A shift in institutional arrangements, with an increasing share of PSE slots subcontracted to nonprofit organizations, also kept the displacement rate down.

2. In terms of job creation, program maintenance uses of PSE accounted for roughly half of the positions located in school districts and the sample governments as of December 1979 and increased generally across all employing agencies between 1979 and 1980. Outside of nonprofit organizations, few participants were providing new services, with expansions of existing services accounting for most of the other job creation uses of PSE.

3. Primarily because of the training requirements in Title II-D, but also because of the ability to supplement wage levels in Title VI, the latter became the preferred title among the sample governments—although, overall, the proportion they retained of both titles declined steadily between 1977 and 1980.

4. Among the sample governments, the extent of displacement was highest in rural areas. In part this reflects the fact that these governments retained higher proportions of their PSE positions, and tended to use them to provide basic services.

5. The proportion of PSE slots used for program maintenance increased with the degree of fiscal pressure, while jurisdictions facing moderate fiscal pressure had the highest displacement rate among positions in the sample governments.

6. Of local funding for which the PSE funds substituted, approximately two-fifths was accounted for by tax stabilization uses.

7. The rest of the funds were split between expenditure in other areas and increased fund balances, each accounting for slightly less than one-fourth of the substitution uses of the funds.

Appendix to Chapter 3
A Statistically Based Analysis of the Job Creation Impact of PSE

As a follow-up to the field evaluation research, a statistical analysis of the job creation impact of PSE was performed for a group of 30 large cities, including some that were covered in the field research and others that were not. The results of that analysis are presented in this section and compared to the findings from the field research and earlier econometric studies of PSE.

Previous Econometric Studies

The most important previous econometric studies on the employment effects of public service employment programs were conducted by George Johnson and James Tomola, starting with PEP, the precursor to CETA-PSE. Johnson and Tomola estimated in a paper presented in 1975 that the displacement rate under PEP rose from 39 percent in the first quarter of the program to 67 percent after two years.[10] A more recent study by the same authors covering public employment under the PEP program and its continuation through the end of 1975 under CETA-PSE estimated displacement at 0 percent after one quarter, 58 percent after one year, and 100 percent after one-and-one-half years.[11]

Among reviewers of this work, there was a consensus that the results were highly volatile depending on the particular specification of the model used. In examining the Johnson and Tomola data, Michael Wiseman estimated that, depending upon the assumptions made, the rate of displacement after one year varied from 0 to 80 percent.[12] Similarly, Michael Borus and Daniel Hamermesh, in a paper for the National Commission on Employment Policy, stressed the volatility of the Johnson-Tomola findings.

We have seen that the precision of the econometric analyses is illusory. The estimates of job creation and fiscal substitution have large confidence bounds so that the actual rates can lie within a very broad range of values. The estimates are based on the assumptions and model specification of their authors. Changes in these assumptions or models will drastically affect the magnitude of job creation and fiscal substitution rates.[13]

In a later study using cross-sectional data on states, cities, and counties, Laurie Bassi and Alan Fechter concluded that, while PSE results in substantial job creation in the short run, over the long run such effects are significantly reduced.[14] In reporting their findings, Bassi and Fechter were careful to note the problems that they, too, encountered in attempting to isolate the independent budgetary effects of PSE. In the case of cities, for example, they attempted to estimate the impact of PSE on real wage expenditures through an equation which included as explanatory variables the real wage bill and local personal income for the previous year, PSE, all other federal grants, and a price index for city wages. Commenting on the results obtained for 1975 and 1976, the authors noted, "Overall the results of these experiments were disappointing . . . The parameters of all the variables were quite unstable, shifting dramatically between 1975 and 1976. When the CETA variable had a plausible parameter, as it did in the 1976 sample, it was statistically insignificant."[15]

Among the complicating factors in the Bassi-Fechter study were the imprecise methods used in estimating the wage bill variable and in combining this variable with the other budgetary data in the model. With respect to measurement, the annual wage bill was estimated by multiplying wages paid in October by a factor of 12. In turn, this calendar-year salary and wage estimate was applied to other budgetary data, which due to the wide range of fiscal-year accounting periods used by cities, varied significantly from city to city as to the calendar-year time periods encompassed.[16]

Additional measurement problems involved estimates of the PSE variable. In particular, failure to appropriately adjust PSE funds received by a city for amounts passed on to other governments or nonprofit agencies through subcontracting arrangements caused the job creation impact estimated on the basis of city wage and salary expenditures to be biased downward.[17]

Integrating Field Research and Statistical Estimation

The statistically based estimates of the job creation impact of PSE undertaken in conjunction with the Brookings-Princeton field research involved pooled time-series data on 30 large cities for the period 1970 through 1979. Before turning to a detailed discussion of the analysis underlying these findings, it is worth noting how the statistical effort improves on earlier attempts to gauge the net job creation impact of PSE and, in particular, how the field network evaluation research provided a more informed basis upon which to structure the statistical analysis.

Avoiding Measurement Error

One contribution of the field research was to help avoid potential measurement error associated with the data used in the statistical analysis. The results of the field research indicated that use of PSE allocations to individual cities (the measure used by Bassi and Fechter) would cause a downward bias in the estimated job creation impact of PSE for two reasons. First, cities subcontracted substantial parts of their PSE money to other jurisdictions and to nonprofit organizations. During the second round of field observations, for example, subcontracting was reported to have accounted for 48 percent of total PSE outlays by the jurisdictions in the field network evaluation study.

A further bias from using allocations data concerns the fact that, as reported by the field associates, the rate at which PSE funds were actually spent varied significantly from city to city, and for each city varied from one time period to another. This information made it clear that reliable net job creation estimates would require city-specific PSE expenditure data rather than data on gross allocations of PSE funds from the Department of Labor.

Model Specification

The current study focuses on the operating side of city budgets. In theory, PSE-related workers could substitute for capital resources, but the field research found no such substitution.

The field research provided further guidance by indicating that any statistical model for gauging the net job creation impact would have to be sensitive to program maintenance uses of PSE—that is, using PSE funds to cushion reductions in local employment. Particularly among the larger and more fiscally distressed cities, the field associates reported substantial use of PSE to ease such cutbacks, and such uses are more likely to be captured in a cross-sectional data base than one based strictly on time-series data.

Additional insights from the field research helped identify appropriate control variables in estimating the net job creation impact of PSE. In particular, the diversity of fiscal circumstances among localities that was reported by the field associates argued strongly for including a fiscal stress variable. It also became obvious that another dimension that would have to be controlled was the variety of organizational structures and range of functional responsibility among large cities.

On balance, the field research suggested that a pooled time-series model using city-specific PSE expenditure data would provide better control for structural differences among cities than had been achieved in earlier cross-sectional studies, as well as greater sensitivity to spending cutbacks than had been achieved in earlier aggregated time-series analyses.

Modeling Salary and Wage Outlays

For this study,[18] the principal dependent variable for gauging the net job creation impact of PSE is salary and wage outlays. To the extent that PSE adds to total employment by large cities, a positive correlation would be expected between PSE funds and these outlays.[19] In order to gauge the independent effects of PSE, however, it is necessary to identify and control for the effects of other factors that have an influence on salaries and wages. For this purpose, an equation was specified consisting of five principal elements.

1. *Per-Capita Personal Income.* This variable controls for the effects of variations in local economies on the provision of local public services. Assuming that community welfare derives from consumption of both private and public goods and services and that communities seek to maximize welfare in relation to available resources, then spending on public services and, in turn, public employment will vary directly with local income.

2. *Per-Capita State Grants, PSE Grants, and Other Federal Grants.* To the extent that such grants add generally to total operating expenditures, one would expect them to also increase salary and wage outlays. With respect to other federal grants we constructed separate series for the 1970-74 period and for the 1975-79 period. This partitioning was made to take account of the changing nature of these grants. In the later period there was a greater emphasis on operating as opposed to capital grants, as well as increased use of a block grant design, which permits greater local discretion in the use of both capital and operating grants.

3. *Fiscal Stress Condition.* The degree of fiscal stress varies considerably among cities. To the extent fiscal stress is related to the propensity of cities to consume public services, the income coefficient in the salary and wage equation will

perform less well as the fiscal stress characteristics of a city depart from the norm. Accordingly, a fiscal stress ranking was included in the equation. Specifically, cities were grouped into four fiscal stress categories, ranging from 1 (low fiscal stress) to 4 (high stress). The ranking was based on each city's fiscal 1975 ratio of unearmarked cash and security holdings (net of outstanding short term debt) to its total general operating outlays.

Per capita wage and salary outlays were observed to vary from an average of $80 for the five cities in the lowest fiscal stress group in 1970 to $187 for the seven cities in the highest fiscal stress group. Over time inflation was likely to exaggerate this gap between high and low fiscal stress cities so we combined the fiscal stress classifications with an inflation index based on the National Income Accounts price deflator for the state and local government sector.

4. *Fiscal Structure.* Because long-run tax and spending behavior may be systematically influenced by differences in local fiscal structures, we included a variable constructed as the ratio of property to total taxes in 1970.[20]

5. *Adjustment for Organizational Differences.* In order to control for the effect of organizational differences among cities on the scope of public services provided and, in turn, the level of salary and wage outlays, a separate site dummy was specified for each city included in the pooled time-series data base.

Data

The salary and wage equation was fitted to a pooled time-series data base for 30 cities covering fiscal 1970 through fiscal 1979. The 30 cities were those for which reliable estimates could be made of direct expenditures of PSE funds for salaries and wages of PSE participants hired by the city itself, as opposed to participants subcontracted to other governments or nonprofit organizations. Information pertaining to PSE spending on city workers was obtained from unpublished worksheets developed by the Governments Division of the Bureau of the Census in conjunction with its annual compilation of revenue and expenditure data for the nation's largest cities.[21]

One shortcoming in the PSE expenditure data derived from the worksheets is the incomplete accounting of PSE-funded expenditures for program administration. Such expenses, including salaries, were limited to 10 percent of the grant. Except for cities that administered their programs through contractual arrangements, such uses show up in PSE-related salary and wage expenditures along with direct expenditures for PSE participants. This shortcoming may cause some downward bias in the estimated net job creation impact of PSE.

Data on the other intergovernmental grant variables, the tax-base composition variable, and the salary and wage outlay variable were taken directly from the computerized data base associated with the annual financial survey conducted by the Governments Division of the Bureau of the Census. The salary and wage variable reflects actual annual outlays and is measured within the same 12-month accounting period as the PSE expenditure variable.

Estimating Procedures

The salary and wage equation was fitted to the pooled time-series data base using an ordinary least squares (OLS) estimating procedure. A crucial assumption in using ordinary least squares is that PSE enters as an exogenous variable and is not a direct function of the salary and wage variable. Based on the nature of the PSE funding formula, this appears to be a reasonable assumption; that is, employment and poverty factors, not spending levels per se, determine each city's allocation. Moreover, a city's allocation and the rate at which it draws down that allocation are highly variable across cities and at different times within a city.

The appropriateness of an OLS estimating procedure was also assessed in terms of the residuals that resulted from fitting the salary and wage equation to the pooled time-series data base. For individual cities, a distinct pattern of successive over- or underprediction was observed in several cases for the period of 1970 to 1976. Of particular concern was the possibility of an inherent tendency toward over- or underprediction during the ensuing 1977-79 period which might bias the estimated PSE impacts. A city-specific time trend variable for those cities whose residuals indicated a strong tendency toward positive serial correlation was included to control this basis.[22] A statistically significant trend was found in seven of the 30 cities, and time trend variables for these cities were included in the final specification.

Estimated Impacts of PSE

The results of fitting the salary and wage equation to the pooled time-series data base are shown in table 3A-1. Turning first to the per capita income variable, a highly significant relationship is indicated with each additional $100 of per-capita personal income estimated to result in an additional $1.30 in local government salary and wage outlays.

A positive and statistically significant distinction is found between the spending patterns and the fiscal stress variable. Cities characterized as under high fiscal stress are estimated to have spent $62 more per capita on salary and wages in 1970 than cities under low fiscal stress. Given an adjustment based on the price deflator for state and local expenditures, the differential increases to $123 by 1979.

The tax composition variable, which reflects the proportion of total taxes in 1970 accounted for by the property tax, exhibits a negative and statistically significant relationship with salary and wage outlays. Specifically, each additional

percentage point decrease in the share of total taxes accounted for by the property tax is estimated to result in an increase of $.85 in per-capita salary and wage outlays.

Table 3A-1
Estimated Salary and Wage Equation
From a Pooled Time-Series Analysis
of Thirty Large Cities, 1970-79

Dependent variables	City salary and wage outlays
Independent variables	
Personal income	+.0130
	(6.42)
Fiscal stress classification	+20.4719
	(7.14)
Property to total taxes, 1970	−.8476
	(3.91)
Other federal grants 1970-74	+.0085
	(0.16)
Other federal grants 1975-79	+.0447
	(1.05)
State grants	+.2753
	(10.79)
Public service employment grants, 1977	+.2994
	(1.58)
Public service employment grants, 1978	+.7669
	(4.34)
Public service employment grants, 1979	+.7140
	(3.34)

NOTES: 1. All economic and budgetary data are in per capita terms.
2. Absolute values of t statistics are in parentheses.
3. Also included in the salary and wage equation, but not reported above were a
series of city-specific place dummies and time trend variables.
4. The other federal grants variables include PSE of PSE-type grants through
fiscal 1976.

There is no evidence of a statistically significant impact from other federal grants in either the 1970-74 period or the 1975-79 period. However, a positive and statistically significant impact on salary and wages was indicated for state grants to cities. Specifically, each additional dollar of state aid is estimated to have resulted in an additional $.28 in salary and wage outlays.

The marked difference between the effect of federal and state grants on city salary and wage outlays partly reflects the compositional differences between the two grant sources; that is, a higher proportion of state grants is devoted to operating uses. A second factor may have to do with the attitudes among cities about the two sources of aid. The results of this analysis strongly suggest that cities were not willing to become dependent on federal aid to support their payrolls. This may be due to the newness during this period of many federal programs geared to operating uses, and perhaps to a perception that the political process that controls federal grant programs is more remote and capricious compared with state-based assistance. This combination of newness and remoteness made federal aid a more uncertain source of revenue.

PSE grants exhibit a much different impact pattern as compared to the other federal grants. For each of the three years, the public service employment program is estimated to have had a stimulative effect on salary and wage outlays by large cities. For 1977, each additional dollar of PSE is estimated to have added $.30 to salary and wage outlays. However, with a t statistic of 1.58, this estimate is only marginally significant. For 1978, the PSE program is estimated to have had a much larger impact, with each additional dollar of PSE adding approximately $.77 to salaries and wages. Similarly, for 1979, each dollar of PSE is estimated to have added $.71 to salary and wage outlays. With t statistics of 4.34 and 3.34 in 1978 and 1979, respectively, these estimates are significant at a 99 percent probability level.[23] This shift to a much larger impact from PSE on salary and wages in 1978 and 1979 is consistent with the large increase in PSE outlays in 1978 and the tightening of the eligibility criteria and other restrictions which would make it more difficult to displace locally funded workers with PSE-funded workers.

Conclusions

The results of this statistical analysis of PSE's impact on salary and wage outlays by large cities in 1977, 1978, and 1979 indicate that the program had a substantial net job creation impact, especially in fiscal years 1978 and 1979. Given the difference in the estimates between these two years and fiscal 1977, these results indicate a substantial effect from the changes in the eligibility criteria and the requirement of a project approach to PSE. This suggests that, to the extent the federal government seeks to promote job creation through the intergovernmental grant system to reduce either cyclical or structural unemployment, any grant similar to PSE should have fairly restrictive eligibility criteria and limits on the types of PSE jobs created.

In relation to earlier econometric research, this current study suggests that with careful attention to the specification of the factors underlying salary and wage behavior (including more refined treatment of intergovernmental revenue and of factors related to fiscal stress, financial management, and institutional differences among cities) and with greater accuracy in the measurement of key variables, better estimates of net expenditure effects can be obtained.

Further, the difference between the 1977 result and those for 1978 and 1979 suggests that earlier concern over differences in findings regarding substitution may have been, at least in part, due to the different time periods and program models for which the estimates were derived.

Finally, the results of this analysis are quite consistent with the Brookings-Princeton field evaluation research. Specifically, the estimate for 1978, indicating that $.77 of each dollar from PSE added to salary and wage outlays, lends statistical reinforcement to the $.78 job creation estimates for large cities derived from the first two rounds of the Brookings-Princeton field research.

NOTES

1. Edward M. Gramlich, "State and Local Budgets the Day After it Rained: Why is the Surplus So High?" *Brookings Papers on Economic Activity,* 1978, no. 1, pp. 191-214.

2. See George Johnson and James Tomola, "The Fiscal Substitution Effect of Alternative Approaches to Public Service Employment Policy," *The Journal of Human Resources,* vol. 12 (Winter 1977), pp. 3-26.

3. See Robert D. Reischauer, "The Economy, the Budget, and Prospects for Urban Aid," in Roy Bahl, ed., *The Fiscal Outlook for Cities* (Syracuse University Press, 1978), p. 104.

4. Unsubsidized employment opportunities generated through displacement uses of PSE are discussed later in this chapter in the section on fiscal effects.

5. "Trend-type" studies refer to extrapolations of employment data as a basis for analyzing the impact of federally aided job programs. Comparing the trend in total state and local employment to the change in the level of PSE, Robert D. Reischauer estimated that during the first nine months of the CETA buildup, the displacement rate was 42 percent. See Reischauer, op. cit.

6. Testimony by George E. Peterson, Hearings before the Subcommittee on the City of the Committee on Banking, Finance, and Urban Affairs of the U.S. House of Representatives and the Joint Economic Committee, July 25, 1978, p. 76.

7. For a discussion of the urban conditions index used to rate urban distress, see Paul R. Dommel and others, *Decentralizing Community Development* (The Brookings Institution, 1978), appendix 2. In brief, an index reading of 100 or above means that a city is more fiscally distressed than the average; the higher the number, the greater the distress. For this analysis, a city with a score of 250 or more was included in the distressed category.

8. For the third and fourth rounds, displacement uses of PSE were reported only on an aggregate basis. This reflected a judgment that the more detailed accounting used in the earlier rounds had not proven sufficiently informative to warrant the additional time and effort involved in providing such detail.

9. In many states, some geographic areas were too sparsely populated to be eligible for status as prime sponsors. These areas were served by a "balance of state" prime sponsor, typically an office within the state labor department, which handled programs in all areas not served by any other prime sponsor.

10. George Johnson and James Tomola, "The Efficacy of Public Service Employment Programs," Technical Analysis Paper No. 17A, Department of Labor, June 1975; processed.

11. George Johnson and James Tomola, "The Fiscal Substitution Effect of Alternative Approaches to Public Service Employment Policy," *The Journal of Human Resources,* vol. 12, no. 1 (Winter 1977), pp. 3-26.

12. Michael Wiseman, "Public Employment as Fiscal Policy," *Brookings Papers on Economic Activity,* no. 1 (1976), pp. 67-114.

13. Michael Borus and Daniel Hamermesh, "Study of the Net Employment Effects of Public Service Employment—Econometric Analyses," in *An Interim Report to the Congress of the National Commission for Manpower Policy, Job Creation Through Public Service Employment,* vol. 3, Commissioned Papers, March 1978, p. 130.

14. Laurie Bassi and Alan Fechter, *The Implications for Fiscal Substitution and Occupational Displacement Under Expanded CETA Title VI,* Technical Analysis Paper No. 65, U.S. Department of Labor, Office of the Assistant Secretary for Policy, Evaluation and Research, March 1979.

15. Ibid., p. 85.

16. The Governments Division of the Bureau of the Census, which is the source of the budgetary data in the Bassi-Fechter study, measures the current fiscal-year accounting period according to budget cycles that close between July 1 of the previous year and June 30 of the current year. Hence, a wage bill estimated for calendar 1975 could be correlated with fiscal 1975 budgetary data compiled over a period ranging from August 1, 1973 to July 31, 1974 or from July 1, 1974 to June 30, 1975.

17. Bassi and Fechter acknowledged this measurement problem and made an upward adjustment to their job creation estimates to compensate for it.

18. For a more detailed discussion of the modeling and estimation procedures used in the pooled time-series analysis, see Charles F. Adams, Jr., Robert F. Cook, and Arthur J. Maurice, "A Pooled Time-Series Analysis of the Job Creation Impact of Public Service Employment Grants to Large Cities," *The Journal of Human Resources,* vol. 18, no. 2 (Spring 1983), pp. 283-294.

19. An alternative specification, using employment levels as the dependent variables, was rejected because the government's data are point-in-time estimates (based on the pay period including October 15) while the financial variables represent fiscal year flows and because PSE-funded jobs are not consistently included in the total employment estimates.

20. Empirical evidence of such an influence is provided by the -.35 correlation (significant at a 94 percent probability level) between the ratio of property to total taxes in 1970 and the percent change in total per-capita taxes from 1970 through 1979 for the thirty cities in the study.

21. Necessary information for identifying city-based uses of PSE as opposed to amounts subcontracted was not available prior to fiscal 1977. In one other case, the salary and wage series behaved erratically over the ten-year period and there were anomalies in some of the other fiscal variables. For these reasons it was dropped, leaving 30 cities.

22. It should be noted that the flow of PSE funds into a city was governed by the rate at which it filled PSE slots. Accordingly, PSE allocations do not accumulate into a city's fund balances and therefore do not require a more complex budgetary model, capable of accounting not only for the effects of current PSE allocations on salary and wages, but also the effects of PSE funds accumulated from prior periods.

23. In comparing these results to those reported earlier from the field research, it should be noted that the fiscal year estimates reported in table 3A-1 are derived from Governments Division data which coincide with accounting periods ending between July 1 of the preceding calendar year and June 30 of the current calendar year. Accordingly, the fiscal 1977 coefficient reflects the impact of PSE during calendar 1976 for some cities, while for others it reflects the impact during the last half of calendar 1976 and the first half of 1977. Hence, the 1977 coefficient predates the estimates from the first and second rounds of the Brookings-Princeton study, which are more appropriately compared with the fiscal 1978 estimate report in table 3A-1. For similar reasons, the fiscal 1979 estimate in table 3A-1 (covering calendar year 1978 for some cities and the period July 1, 1978 to June 30, 1979 for others) cannot be directly compared to either of the two subsequent field observations in December 1979 and December 1980.

4

Public Service Employment as Training Policy

The previous chapter presented evidence that public service job programs can fulfill one of the goals that has been put forth for them: to create jobs quickly and relatively efficiently. The picture is less clear, however, when we ask about the lasting effects of the program on the vast numbers of people who held those publicly funded jobs.

In the decade from 1971 to 1981, millions of people held PSE jobs. It is reasonable to expect that this job experience resulted in some training of participants. The one study of net post-program experience that has been done for PSE participants who entered the program in FY 1976 indicates that PSE generated about $300 per year in average earnings gains for participants in the first two years following their participation in the program. This represents about a 6 percent gain in earnings relative to what they would have earned in the absence of the program and is equal to the average for all CETA participants.[1] This is an average result for all participants who entered in that period of time. No study has been done that relates post-program experience to the kinds of jobs and the amount of training that particular participants received. However, the results of the field research provide some indication of the kind of training provided to whom and the likely longer run effects of that experience.

The information that is available enables us to examine many aspects of how the PSE programs of the 1970s affected participants. This information is particularly valuable not only because a large number of persons participated in the program, offering a solid data base, but also because the several changes in program design and in political and economic circumstances enable us to assess how these changes related to program outcomes.

Unlike many other federally supported training programs, PSE provided training largely as a side effect of the jobs it provided. Because most job training in the United States takes place on the job, however, there is little question that PSE jobs, with or without supplemental training, could help participants develop both general and specific job skills. Not all work experience is equally valuable, of course, so a major question is whether the program as it was implemented met some minimal criteria for effective training.

Chief among these criteria is that the program must enroll those who can make gains from the experience. Next, the participants should be effectively matched with training opportunities. This is a particularly difficult step because both the job level and the characteristics of participants are influenced by policy changes such as altering the participant eligibility requirements or setting a maximum wage. If participants are already fully trained for the positions they hold—or, at the other extreme, if they are so ill-prepared that they cannot learn the jobs—then the on-the-job training gains will not be great. Finally, if a program is to succeed, the jobs must require skills that will be useful in obtaining unsubsidized employment. PSE would fail as an effective training program if it succeeded only in training the equivalent of the proverbial buggy whip makers!

Matching Needs with Opportunities

A critical feature of the PSE program under CETA was the attempt to target positions to those who would otherwise be unemployed and who could also make significant long term gains from involvement with the program. By adjusting the eligibility regulations, the federal government attempted to fine tune the program to both attain maximum training effectiveness and stimulate the economy without creating inflation.

The theoretical case for this targeting rests indirectly on the notion that there are frictions, immobilities, and rigidities in the labor market which prevent the free and instantaneous adjustment of wages and employment to current labor market conditions. Such imperfections mean that when labor market conditions change—as when demand for some occupation goes down while demand for other occupations rises—the result will be not just changes in wages for the different occupations but also unemployment. The unemployment will be concentrated in certain geographic areas, among unskilled workers, or among persons who are discriminated against in some way.

The relatively high unemployment rates of certain groups is evidence that such target groups exist. Minorities, persons with less than a high school education, and teenagers are much more likely to be unemployed than are whites of prime working age. Even when members of these groups are employed, they are much more likely to hold unskilled, low-paying jobs.

Several theories about the labor market have been offered to explain these obervations. These theories differ in many respects, but they all agree that those with few or no skills are more likely to be unemployed or frequently laid off while those with high levels of skill are in greater demand.

One such theory stresses the importance of restrictions on wages, especially laws setting a minimum wage. According to this theory, if Congress or a legislature sets a minimum wage that is higher than some employers are willing to pay for certain jobs and some workers are willing to accept lower wages for those jobs, then fewer jobs will be available. If the number of people seeking jobs exceeds the number of available jobs, employers will hire those with greater skills and leave the least skilled without jobs.

A different approach leading to a similar conclusion is taken by those who see the labor market as segmented. Workers in the lowest-status jobs, in this view, are unable to move up because they lack education and training, or because they face discrimination, or because their behavior is unsuited to the demands of better jobs, or for all of these reasons. Because they are hired only for low-skilled jobs, they cannot obtain on-the-job training that will help them break out of their inferior status. The forces that keep these people in low-paid jobs—what is known as the secondary sector of the labor market—can create an excess of labor in this sector even when skilled jobs are available.

Both these theories agree that the high unemployment rates among teenagers, minorities, and unskilled workers are due to involuntary unemployment. There are, however, some who staunchly maintain that voluntary turnover explains these rates, and that unemployment among these groups would be reduced if the market were allowed to work without restriction. This type of argument is based either on the view that market imperfections are not significant or on the contention that the proposed cures are worse than the problems.

This is not the place to settle the differences among these theories. It is important to recognize, however, that the case for targeting rests heavily on the proposition that there is involuntary unemployment, and that those who are involuntarily unemployed face structural labor market barriers and lack skills needed for available jobs. A job creation program for these workers does not create inflationary pressures or draw workers into public employment at the expense of the private sector. This condition makes public service employment desirable as a countercyclical job creation remedy.

Since the same people are experiencing severe labor market difficulties, they also stand to gain from the job experience. Thus, targeting to those who have low earnings and a history of unemployment is often supported as both a counter-cyclical and structural policy objective.

The theoretical defense for targeting is relatively simple compared to the problems faced in actually defining and reaching a target group. At the point of implementation one must abandon references to structural unemployment, unskilled labor, and the economically disadvantaged in favor of some measurable characteristics that can be used to determine who is and who is not eligible for programs. One approach is to use race, sex, and age as criteria. Although a relatively high proportion of some population groups may experience labor market difficulties, simply being a member of the demographic group is not sufficient evidence of need. In order for PSE to be effective as a training program, it should be aimed at those with relatively low incomes and a high probability of unemployment, regardless of economic conditions. This means the program must use eligibility requirements that indicate individual labor market problems.

Even among those who experience difficulties in the labor market there are important differences in need and ability to benefit from training. The notion of targeting may be clarified if we think in terms of labor market layers or segments which, while not rigorously defined, are conceptually useful.[2] At the top are those workers who hold regular jobs and do not require any special labor market assistance. The second tier could be those who have some skills and often hold good jobs but who are the first to be laid off in a recession. This could be the case because of lack of seniority, employment in cyclically sensitive industries such as building construction, or relatively low skill. Their need for assistance is usually brief and may be met by income transfers or temporary employment.

At the third level are those workers who experience more difficult long term problems. They are unable to secure permanent employment because they lack job skills, because they face discrimination, or because they do not know where to look for jobs that may be open to them. People in these circumstances are likely to have low incomes and periodic long stretches of unemployment even in prosperous times. Even though they may have adequate basic education and are willing to work, they need training and job exposure that will given them entry to more stable employment.

The very bottom layer of the labor pool consists of those who lack the basic skills necessary for holding permanent jobs. Their deficiencies may extend to communication skills and the ability to work independently. In some cases they may have attitudinal or emotional problems that stand in the way of holding good jobs. Such workers are most in need of highly structured programs in remedial education, basic work habits, or rudimentary job skills.

Our observations of the PSE program over several years and in a variety of jurisdictions lead us to the conclusion that matching participants with positions for the purpose of training is one of the most difficult policy objectives to implement. Generally, it is our opinion that the most appropriate target group for a PSE program is the third labor market layer. The top two groups do not need the training that can be readily provided through public employment, and the bottom layer needs training that is best provided in another setting. After all, PSE participants must be able to hold jobs. From observing the system in action we have also come to believe that the questions of who should be involved and how they can best be reached in a decentralized system were both misunderstood and confused with other program purposes. The following sections trace our observations during two distinct phases of the program's history.

PSE as a Training Program, 1976-78

As the previous chapters explained, the lessons to be drawn from the PSE program can best be understood if we look at three distinct phases: one before 1976, when eligibility rules were loose; a second between 1976 and 1979, when new rules imposed some targeting; and the final phase after 1979, when the stringent eligibility requirements enacted in 1978 took effect and limited the program to those with low skills and long histories of unemployment.

Before 1976, PSE probably drew most of its enrollees from the first and second tiers of the labor market. Some excellent training opportunities were created during this time, but it is our conclusion that most participants did not really need training to locate and hold permanent jobs.

The story of PSE as a training effort thus begins in 1976, when Congress created the short term "projects" segment of the program and introduced eligibility requirements, shifting the program's emphasis toward the long term unemployed. During this period, as noted in chapter 2, local governments created jobs in a wide range of occupations and in several important functional areas. This distribution by occupation and function suggests that many jobs were created requiring skills that could be used in regular unsubsidized employment.

Further, most PSE participants during this period were assigned to real jobs in regular local government departments, rather than to training programs. In fact, as discussed in chapter 2, the services provided by these local areas were highly valued by the local officials. Because little formal training was provided, we must look at the effects of on-the-job experience.

The general types of PSE experiences fall into three categories, each of which has definite implications with respect to training. First, many jurisdictions hired well-qualified people to fill positions that helped the jurisdiction meet public service needs. Unemployment was high in most of the sample areas and limits on wages and tenure were loose. As a result, PSE participants were most often chosen from a pool of applicants based strictly on their ability to perform the needed tasks. Since the pool of applicants exceeded the numberof jobs, usually by a factor of five or more, some local governments tried to "cream" the target group, selecting workers from what we would generally define as the second tier of the labor market. That is, most PSE participants needed temporary employment, not training.

The second category consisted of jobs tailored for more disadvantaged persons, but still with the objective of filling important jobs. These positions were valued by local jurisdictions, but did not require high skill levels. This was the situation for a majority of the positions in our sample areas during the 1976-78 period. There was a strong emphasis on informal training for these positions; local jurisdictions frequently provided extra supervision or other job-related aid to help the PSE participants perform at an acceptable level.

Finally, a significant number of positions were designed strictly to absorb eligible participants. The chief objective was to keep people busy at the least possible additional cost to the local jurisdiction. There were few standards for this type of employment beyond the ability to "show up on time," and even this requirement was often relaxed. Officials in many jurisdictions considered hiring some unskilled persons to be the price for getting other workers who could be used in highly valued public services. These jurisdictions practiced program segmentation, using one part of PSE (usually the sustainment portion as explained in chapter 1) to fill skilled positions, and the projects portion to place unskilled persons.

Because local government had no incentive to provide supplemental institutional training to the participants, the best
training opportunities existed where the jobs were of importance to the locality and where supervisors were therefore
directly concerned with the quality of the work. Many
associates reported that the dead-end jobs with no regular
workforce contact which were created for the most disadvantaged tended to have little relevance for future employment
and may even have stigmatized the participants. But this type
of employment was held to a minimum in the PSE program
of 1976-78 because local governments had a strong interest in
the performance level of PSE employees who held these positions and made an effort to supervise the employees and to
provide them with on-the-job training. Very early in our
studies we saw that there was a major difficulty in targeting
positions to those who can benefit from the training without
going so far down the queue that the employer simply gives
up and decides that a simple work experience program for
the unskilled is all that can reasonably be managed.

Was PSE a good training program in 1976-78? In answer-
ing that question we should remember that job creation, not
job training, was the primary program objective at the time.
Furthermore, since there was very little formal training for
the participants there is little to observe except the job experience. The PSE field associates made considerable effort
to ascertain the extent to which participants were matched
with jobs for the purpose of developing the participants'
potential. But most jurisdictions had no discernible training
policy of any type.

Even though findings on training under these circumstances are somewhat inconclusive, the thousands of interviews with local officials, program operators, and CETA
participants led us to the conclusion that out of the conflict
between the targeting and job creation objectives of PSE,
program aspects emerged which strengthened the program as

a training experience. As local governments attempted to use PSE to provide needed public services while drawing the employees from among eligible persons, the governments found it necessary to provide a considerable amount of instruction in job skills. This beneficial result could not have existed if the pressure on targeting became so great that the cost of training exceeded the value of the services, or if wage limitations or other restrictions on job types prevented the local governments from creating PSE jobs in regular government departments.

After assessing the reports of associates in 1977 we found that PSE was an attractive program for unemployed but trainable people who were willing to accept short term employment in the public sector. Many of the jobs created in this program gave participants the chance to move into permanent positions with the employing agency.

We also found that many employers had been pleasantly surprised at the quality of the program participants. They reported no difficulty in filling the positions with suitable workers who met the 1976 eligibility requirements. Of course, this was not the case in every jurisdiction. Some localities successfully avoided the population needing training, even under rather stringent requirements for eligibility. Others developed two-tier programs where the good training opportunities were reserved for those who really did not need training while the needy were shunted off to positions with little opportunity. But in spite of the fact that very few areas had programs that showed any direct concern for the training needs of participants, the picture was brighter than it seemed at first glance. Training is just as effective when it is done out of concern for the output as when it is done out of concern for the participants.

In some high-wage areas we also began to see what would become a typical case as the program was further restricted. Where the allowable PSE wage was below the standard wage in traditional government departments, there was little opportunity to create regular positions for the disadvantaged.

In a few jurisdictions where the wage was not a problem, there was such a negative response to all federal programs that PSE was never productively used. In these areas the program gravitated to the status of a relief program for the poor. The jobs created as a result of the PSE grant under these circumstances were largely cleanup projects or simple repair and maintenance work. While these may have been of temporary value to the community, they offered little in the way of training.

As we have emphasized throughout, PSE was not one program but many different programs, differing substantively across jurisdictions and over time. This fact becomes most clear when we consider PSE's training aspects. Even so, with the above background in mind, we can make some general conclusions about the drift of training in PSE as the program regulations changed.

The tightening of restrictions in the 1976 CETA reauthorization pushed the program further down the labor queue. Wage and other limitations helped generate more positions for unskilled and semiskilled workers. In most jurisdictions, however, enough slack remained to enable officials to create jobs in regular government departments where the participants would help provide valued services. It is our judgment that this balancing of interests was effective for the promotion of on-the-job training, although very little supplemental skill training was provided. Certainly, the absence of formal training programs in connection with PSE was one of the chief reasons Congress in 1978 attempted to make more of a training program out of PSE.

The Beginning of the End, 1979-80

The 1978 amendments to CETA were more than a simple extension of the previous trends; they forced fundamental program changes. Motivated by data showing that PSE did not draw most of its participants from the bottom tier of the labor market and that very little supplemental training was provided to PSE job holders, Congress in 1978 increased the training emphasis by requiring more identifiable training for those in the bottom labor market tiers. The most important provisions of the amendments were:

1. Tightening the eligibility requirements to screen out those who would be likely to find unsubsidized employment on their own.

2. Lowering the maximum wage and tenure limitations to reduce the attractiveness of PSE positions as alternatives to private employment.

3. Requiring prime sponsors to spend a minimum percentage of the PSE allocation (up to 20 percent of the Title II-D grant) on training activities other than informal on-the-job training.

4. Requiring that an Employability Development Plan (EDP) be prepared for each PSE participant, which would constitute a plan for moving the person through a combination of training and work experience to some permanent unsubsidized job.

Perhaps the easiest effect to observe was the change in the characteristics of the participants, which were shown in chapter 2. A growing proportion of the PSE population was drawn from those population segments that historically have had greatest need of job-skills training. These include minorities, those with less than 12 years of education, and welfare recipients. Many observers saw these as positive changes because they reflected a growing program emphasis on the most disadvantaged segments of the population. Yet in many areas, particularly the large urban labor markets where the highest proportions of these same groups were recruited, a majority of the field associates saw this change as having a negative impact on training.

It appears that the program was now aimed too low. The field associates confirmed our conjecture that, although PSE was an appropriate program to provide job skills for many of the unemployed, it was not suitable for those who lacked basic work and communication skills. In three-fourths of the large cities in our sample of PSE jurisdictions, the field associates reported significant difficulties in finding a training program that the target group could handle. Employers had problems with the dual challenge of keeping the participants interested in the jobs while finding training courses that would noticeably improve their long-run labor market chances. Too many of the participants showed little interest in training, lacking the basic skills for entry to the programs and often refusing to attend. Two quotations from associate reports are typical of the findings:

> On-the-job training, job development, or classroom training cannot compensate for the participants' low level of achievement when entering the program. As a result, the training is virtually ineffective.

* * *

> Because of widespread deficiencies among participants, there was a heavy concentration on attitude, appearance, and basic language training. These were not sufficient to make the target group employable.

With the 1978 amendments, Congress apparently intended that the targeting and training objectives would reinforce each other, but in the large cities just described the two objectives appear to have been in conflict. The type of training that can be successfully linked with PSE-style employment in government or nonprofit agencies proved not to be a solution to the employment problems of the most disadvantaged. In fact, our overall assessment of the PSE training component in large cities after the passage of the 1978 amendments was that it did not meet the basic criteria for a good training program. Because of the deficiencies of the participants and the lack of job opportunities that would provide good training, there was a near certainty of failure for on-the-job training.

In spite of the difficulties, and in compliance with the law, there was an increase in formal training for the disadvantaged. The actual content of this training will be discussed in the next section of this chapter. It is our judgment, however, that these training gains were more than offset by the losses in informal on-the-job training.

In some jurisdictions the amendments had less effect, particularly in small and more rural jurisdictions where the maximum PSE wage was close to or less than prevailing local government wages for some occupations. Many of these jurisdictions were able to continue hiring well-qualified participants and placing them in government positions where they could work with regular government employees and have a chance of gaining a permanent job through turnover or expansion of the local government labor force. Even in these jurisdictions, however, the field associates expressed the opinion that the targeting and wage restrictions had reduced the potential value of PSE as preparation for long term employment. Again we turn to the reports for elaboration:

> With some success, training was linked to the PSE job. However, targeting seems to have pushed the program down to those who lack motivation to complete the program.

* * *

> The program is geared to the most disadvantaged, who need training in proper work habits. This requires extra supervision on the job which the government cannot afford to provide.

In altering PSE to make it more of a traditional "man-power program," Congress generated a system that was plagued by the same dilemma that faced the profusion of alphabet soup training programs for the disadvantaged in the 1960s and 1970s. For workers who have limited work experience, education, and motivation, inexpensive short term training simply does not lead to permanent employment in good jobs. Yet taxpayers are assumed to be unwilling to pay for extended and expensive training. A quick fix for high unemployment among the unskilled remains elusive. When seen in this context, the failure of PSE as a training program for the disadvantaged is understandable.

It should be added that PSE as a program linking training with work experience was never given a fair trial. The training provisions were accompanied with such restrictive participant eligibility requirements and cost restrictions that the system was put under a tremendous strain. Before there was much opportunity to make an adjustment, the program was cancelled. One legacy of PSE is the frustration among local officials resulting from the frequent changes in program goals, federal regulations, the level of funding, and the general lack of appreciation for local circumstances.

The changes brought about by the 1978 amendments were a good example of the disruptions that local governments came to expect in the nine-year CETA experience. Before 1979, formal training was not required for participants, and most workers needed only the informal training they obtained on the job. The 1978 changes were an attempt to graft formal training to this process. But institutional arrangements and expectations cannot be expected to change quickly. Employers understandably resisted the shift from what they considered to be a perfectly adequate arrangement for enhancing their workforce to an emphasis on employees who were untrained, somewhat difficult to manage, and had to be given time off for training.

Formal Training and PSE

In spite of the negative feelings that local officials had toward the 1978 amendments, most made an effort to comply with the provisions specifying that a certain portion of the PSE grant be spent for formal training. In the fourth and final round of the field network study, associates examined the extent of this training by looking at a sample of 50 participants in each jurisdiction. To make the sampling procedure manageable, we first selected a random sample of employing agencies from each jurisdiction, stratified by PSE title and type of agency to reflect the local mix of PSE employers. We then chose a random sample of participants from among those in the sample agencies. We initially wanted a sample of 50 participants per jurisdiction for a total sample of 2,000. Because some smaller jurisdictions did not currently have 50 PSE participants, the eventual sample was 1,940.

Information from the sample participants' files was combined with interviews with agency supervisors to provide four types of information:

1. Personal characteristics, including sex, age, race, and education; whether the participant was economically disadvantaged and was in a family that received public assistance; and the number of weeks the person had been unemployd before entering the program.

2. Type of PSE employer (government, school district, nonprofit organization, etc.), occupation of employment, and wage.

3. Type and length of PSE training, including details on the specific occupation for which the training was conducted. For those participants who received more than one type of training, each type was identified, as well as the sequence in which they occurred.

4. Analysis of the likelihood that the training would lead
   to direct absorption into employment with the PSE
   employing agency or significantly increase the
   likelihood of placement elsewhere.

The training for PSE participants was grouped into three
categories: basic, specific, and general.

Basic training includes motivational training, self-
assessment, life skills, assertiveness, time management, and
the like, as well as training in job search and job interviewing
skills.

Specific training is skills training for specific occupations.
The most common training programs in this category are for
clerical and craft occupations, although we identified more
than 50 different types of specific training. The list of occupations ranged from bartender and radio broadcaster to
carpenter and truck driver. The majority of occupations
were in the traditionally lower-paid categories. For many
participants, some basic training was combined with specific
training. Tables 4-1 through 4-4 show these combinations, as
well as a multiple skills training category for participants
receiving more than one type of specific training. A majority
of the participants in the multiple skills category had either
clerical or craft training as one of the types.

General training includes courses that we would common-
ly classify as "education." Courses for high school or college credit, English as a second language, and adult basic
education made up the bulk of general training.

Type and Length of Training

Table 4-1 shows the distribution of participants by type of
training for the total sample and separately for each type of
jurisdiction. The percentages in the tables are for the column
totals; for example, the 32 percent at the top of the second

Table 4-1
Percentage of Participants by Type of Training and Type of Jurisdiction for Participants Enrolled as of December 1980

Type of training	Total sample	Type of jurisdiction			
		Large distressed cities	Other large cities	Small cities and suburban counties	Rural areas
None	37	32	36	33	47
Basic only	29	31	34	28	23
Skills total	30	31	26	34	25
Clerical	3	4	2	3	4
Basic + clerical	4	1	6	5	2
Subtotal...............	7	5	8	8	7
Health and social services ..	3	3	1	3	3
Basic + health and social services	2	0	3	4	1
Subtotal...............	5	3	4	7	4
Craft	5	9	2	4	6
Basic + craft	3	4	5	2	1
Subtotal...............	8	13	7	6	7
Multiple skills...........	6	3	5	8	5
Other skills	4	7	2	5	2
General total	5	6	4	5	5
General	3	5	3	2	3
Basic + general	2	2	1	3	2
Participant sample size	1,940	399	393	687	461

column indicates that this percentage of the sample participants in the large distressed cities got no training.

Some form of training was provided to about five participants out of eight (63.3 percent) although what was provided was often quite limited. This confirms the summary analysis of the associates, who noted that in many cases participants were simply assigned to the PSE job. That is, the requirement that a certain percentage of the funds be used for training was not interpreted as a requirement that every participant receive training. Reasons for this vary, but associates have noted that where the participant filled a regular government position, agencies had trouble scheduling released time for the worker to attend training sessions. Also, many of the participants in these jobs did not wish to be enrolled in supplemental training courses. In other cases no relevant training opportunities were available in the community.

Although the percentage receiving training was quite uniform across most other jurisdictional types, it was substantially lower than average (53 percent) in the rural governments. As noted earlier, the PSE program in rural areas was less influenced by wage restrictions than in other jurisdictions because community wage levels were lower than these areas were not as likely to be affected by union or civil service wage scales. Here the program continued to be used extensively as a supplement to basic government services. The lower percentage of rural participants who received training is consistent with our hypothesis that training would be less important where the program could still be used to provide important local services.

More than one-quarter of the sample, or 45 percent of those who were in some type of training, received only basic training. Of those who had only basic training, 54 percent had training for one day or less and 93 percent had training for ten days or less. Thus for each type of jurisdiction, 40 percent or fewer of the participants either had any training or had only basic training for a few hours or days. This is a critical finding since it bears directly on the question of how much "real" training was given.[3]

These findings are supported by the associates' narrative analyses. With some exceptions, the associates found that a minority of the participants were provided substantive skill training. One associate summed up what seems to have been a typical situation:

> Some participants are placed in skill training programs but most are simply required to attend classes in attitude, language, and appearance training. While this may be needed, it is not enough to make the target group employable.

Those participants involved in specific skills training had jobs in a wide variety of occupational categories, but were clustered in typing, bookkeeping, the traditional crafts, nursing, and counseling. Only about 5 percent of all participants were enrolled in general training courses, and the vast majority of these were in courses for high school or college credit.

Table 4-2 shows the differences in type of training by the personal characteristics of the trainees, including whether they were welfare recipients. Women were significantly more likely to get training than men, and those who were receiving public assistance had a higher probability of being in training programs than those who were not. Differences by race and age were not significant in most categories.

The most highly educated participants, especially the 7 percent who held college degrees, were the least likely to receive any skill training. If they were trained, it was seldom in the otherwise popular clerical and craft courses. One other significant although not surprising finding is that while males dominated the training in crafts, relatively few received clerical training.

Table 4-2
Type of Training by Personal Characteristics
(percentages)

Type of training	Sex		Race		Age			Years of education				Receive public assistance	
	M	F	White	Non-white	Under 22	22-44	45 and over	Under 12	12	13-15	Over 16	Yes	No
None	41	33	36	38	35	38	36	33	37	39	44	31	39
Basic only	30	28	30	28	30	28	31	30	28	29	32	26	30
Skills total	26	34	30	28	31	30	26	28	32	30	21	35	26
Clerical	1	6	3	3	4	3	2	2	4	4	0	5	2
Basic+clerical	*	7	4	3	5	3	3	2	5	4	2	6	2
Subtotal clerical	1	13	7	6	9	6	5	4	9	8	2	11	4
Health & social services	3	3	2	3	2	3	1	1	3	4	2	3	3
Basic+health & social services	1	3	2	2	2	3	1	2	2	3	2	2	2
Subtotal health & social services	4	6	4	5	4	6	2	3	5	7	4	5	5
Craft	9	2	5	6	7	5	3	7	6	4	0	6	5
Basic+craft	4	1	2	4	3	3	3	5	2	1	1	3	3
Subtotal craft	13	3	7	10	10	8	6	12	8	5	1	9	8
Multiple skills	4	8	8	4	5	6	7	6	6	6	5	7	5
Other skills	4	4	4	3	3	4	6	3	4	4	9	3	4
General total	4	7	4	6	6	6	5	9	3	3	4	9	4
General	2	4	2	4	4	3	4	6	1	3	2	6	2
Basic+general	2	3	2	2	2	3	1	3	2	*	2	3	2
Participant sample size	989	951	904	1,025	467	1,223	235	632	820	322	135	618	1,305

NOTE: Some totals may not add due to missing data in some categories.

*Indicates less than 0.5 percent.

The most highly educated and least disadvantaged participants, especially those who were not from families receiving welfare payments, were less likely to get job training. This is explained by the fact that the most highly qualified were placed in the best PSE jobs while the more disadvantaged were relegated to a combination of low-skill work and training.

Less than two-thirds of the sample received any training, of whom nearly half (30 percent of the total sample) received only brief basic training. Thirty percent of the sample got skill training, concentrated in the clerical and craft skills, while another 5 percent received some general training. By type of jurisdiction, the major difference was that rural jurisdictions had a much higher proportion of participants with no training and a lower proportion receiving only basic training.

Table 4-3 shows length of training by major training activity. As expected, those who had only a short training program—one to ten days—had mostly basic training. Almost every jurisdiction in our sample had some short courses to motivate participants, emphasize the importance of good work habits, or point out some of the problems encountered by people seeking jobs. In one-third of the sample jurisdictions, something of this sort had been set up just to "spend the training dollars." Many private training agencies established special short courses of this type and sold them to local governments as a package. In these courses the participant would typically get a few hours of orientation, testing for skills and interests, and a motivation seminar before being assigned to the PSE position. Although the associates generally agreed that the target group needed the basic skills and motivation that the short courses were designed to improve, none felt that the existing programs of this type would do much to provide those skills.

At the other end of the spectrum, 21 percent of the sample had training for more than 30 days. About two-thirds of these participants were in clerical, craft, or multiple skills programs. According to the narrative descriptions of these programs, many of those in extended skill-training programs were working in PSE positions where the work was related to their training. Three-fourths of the associates identified this as the most successful PSE training strategy; at the same time they pointed out that local governments did not have the money, the opportunity, or the incentive to operate a program of this type for a majority of the participants. Our analysis also showed that the participants with extended skill training were about evenly spread across all types of jurisdictions.

Table 4-3
Percentage of Participants by Length of Training
and Major Training Type
(percentage of those receiving given length of training)

		Number of days of training			
Type of training	None	1 or less	2-10	10-30	More than 30
None	100	--	--	--	--
Basic only	--	96	68	20	1
Skills total	--	4	30	67	83
Clerical	--	--	7	11	23
Health and social service	--	3	9	12	8
Craft	--	--	6	15	26
Multiple	--	--	3	18	17
Other	--	*	5	11	9
General	--	--	3	13	16
Sample size	702	300	330	193	415
(Total sample = 1,940)					

*Indicates less than 0.5 percent.

Training Impact

Ideally, an assessment of the effects of training would include longitudinal data for each participant so that we could determine post-training employment experience. Because this was not possible for a study of this type and has proved difficult even in those studies where the major objectives was to secure follow-up data, we approached the question of training impact in a different way.

For each sample participant, the associates assessed the degree to which formal or informal training in PSE appeared likely to improve the potential for transition to an unsubsidized job. They were asked to consider two major factors in this assessment: (1) whether the training was of the type that might have a positive impact on employability, and (2) whether the participant successfully completed the training. Even though these are qualitative data, they provide considerable insight that cannot be gained by looking only at training time or considering only aggregate data.

The associates concluded that formal or informal training provided as part of a PSE job improved the labor market potential of 1,287 of the 1,940 sample participants (66 percent). They were uncertain about another 431 (22 percent) and said that there was no improvement for only 222 (11 percent). Of those who showed no improvement, 86 percent had no formal training or only basic training.

Table 4-4 shows the percentages, by personal characteristics, of those who were judged not to have improved their labor market potential as a result of having a PSE job relative to the percentage with that characteristic for the total sample. Males, minorities, and those not receiving AFDC were less likely to have improved their labor market potential. We found no significant differences between types of jurisdictions. When we compared types of PSE employers, the only difference we found was that participants employed in nonprofit organizations had a slightly higher change of improving employability.

Given the low level of formal training for most participants (a majority got one day or less), the estimated positive impact on job market potential suggests that informal OJT remains an important part of the training in PSE.

Table 4-4
Characteristics of Participants
Not Improving Labor Market Potential
and Percentages of Total Sample

Characteristic	Not improving labor market potential	Total sample
Sex		
Male	64	51
Female	36	49
Race		
White	35	47
Nonwhite	65	53
Age		
Under 22 years	24	24
22-45 years	57	63
More than 45 years	18	12
Years of schooling		
Less than 12	43	33
12	38	42
More than 12	19	24
Member of family receiving AFDC		
Yes..........................	23	32
No	77	67
Overall average, total sample ..	12	100

The chance that PSE participants would be hired by the agency in which they worked during their program involvement, which we call direct absorption, has always been an important feature of PSE. In the 1980-81 study round, direct absorption was considered highly likely for only 20 percent of the training sample. Females, whites, and persons between 22 and 44 years of age had a greater likelihood of direct absorption than males, nonwhites, and the younger or older participants. Before the 1978 amendments, when the chief local objectives for PSE were the provision of public services and fiscal relief, direct absorption was probably much higher. In fact, in earlier rounds we found that a major criterion for allocating PSE slots was the potential for direct absorption. But the targeting, wage, and tenure limitations of the 1978 amendments reduced the incentive for many of these agencies to participate in the program. The declining direct absorption rate seems to have resulted from local governments' difficulty in creating positions that were useful to them but still met the federal requirements.

Even so, the most common experience for PSE participants who entered employment immediately after leaving the program was to find a job in the agency that had employed them while in the program. In the third round of the study we found that in three-quarters of the sample jurisdictions, retention of PSE participants by employing agencies was the most common type of job placement for former participants. This finding is supported by the Continuous Longitudinal Manpower Survey (CLMS), sponsored by the U.S. Department of Labor, which found that 78 percent of a 1975 cohort of participants who were employed immediately after termination had located jobs in the public sector.

On balance it does not appear that the program design mixing formal training and public service jobs was very successful. However, there were so many changes in PSE during this period that it would not be appropriate to conclude that it has no promise. Many of the field associates felt that if it had been given time and if employers had had a little more latitude in the creation of jobs and selection of participants, the 1979-80 version of PSE may have been a good approach to training. Almost before it was in place there were rumors of more reductions and changes. Therefore, we cannot be certain of the consequences of such a program had it been initiated with full government support and kept in place long enough to work out some of the problems.

We did learn that many participants wanted the jobs but not the training. They did not feel that the short training courses offered in most areas would be of much value. Another problem arose because employers did not want to bother with employees whose work schedule had to be especially arranged to accommodate training. For these and other reasons, the program simply failed to generate the energy and enthusiasm that was characteristic of PSE in 1976-78.

Conclusion

Many of the findings about PSE as a training program are not surprising. Since PSE was employment, the most important training was obtained on the job. The amount and quality of training depended on the nature of the job, the preparation and attitude of the employee, and the importance attached to the job by the employer. Getting the right mix of these factors proved difficult. We concluded that the early PSE program, before 1976, failed as a training program chiefly because most of the employees did not need training. Also, we feel that the program after 1978 was not very successful because the jobs had too little skill content, the participants were not prepared for training, and the employers did not care much about the outcome.

For the interim period, 1976-78, PSE gets relatively high marks as a training program. Somewhat ironically, this was a period when training was a secondary objective and job creation was the major purpose. We learn from this experience that creation of a training environment requires attention to all of the necessary components. Almost by accident, there was in 1976-78 a good pool of trainees, real and important jobs to be learned, and employers who cared about getting the workers trained. While it may have been admirable to attempt to push the program to a more disad-

vantaged population or to save money by limiting the maximum wage, PSE should be seen as an entity where all the
characteristics were interdependent. This institutional or
holistic approach to the analysis does not yield startling
results but provides conclusions that apparently were not
foreseen by those policymakers who, for ten years, seemed
to tamper with the program on the assumption that they
could change one program aspect at a time.

A program such as PSE can provide training if we do not
burden the program by asking it to serve incompatible objectives. While it will never be the best program for the most
disadvantaged, there are many others who need job training,
work experience, and an opportunity for upward mobility.
During the 1970s and early 1980s when unemployment rates
stayed at historically high levels, the opportunities for job
shifting and upward mobility were very limited, especially
for the semiskilled, dislocated workers, and young entrants
to the labor force. Also, none of our current labor market
policies specifically addresses this growing problem.

NOTES

1. Westate, Inc., Net Impact Report No. 1 (Supplement No. 1), *The Impact of CETA on 1978 Earnings: Participants in Selected Program Activities Who Entered CETA During FY 1976,* Office of Program Evaluation, U.S. Department of Labor, Washington, July 1982, Table 3-1, pp.
3-9.

2. The notion of labor market layers is developed in *Public Service
Employment: A Field Evaluation* by Richard P. Nathan, Robert F.
Cook, and V. Lane Rawlins. The Brookings Institution, 1981, pp. 37-38.

3. It should be noted that some of these results may be affected by the
way in which the sample was drawn. The sample was made up of participants who had not terminated by December 31, 1980. Therefore,
training that tends to be up front (such as orientation or basic skills) may
be accurately reported, while back-end training (such as job search skills)
may be somewhat underreported. Similarly, the amount of longer term
training (skill or general) may be understated.

5
Conclusions

Local experience with public service employment differed in many ways owing to differences in size and fiscal conditions of localities as well as to the personalities of program managers. In one rural southern site, the PSE program was shaped by a CETA director who personally knew every employer and PSE participant; in large cities, by contrast, PSE was run by sizable bureaucracies. In one county the board of commissioners became directly involved in PSE to the point that jobs were filled with an eye to political impact. There were also reports of political abuse. In most areas, however, the goals of providing services and helping participants took precedence over heavy handed political expediency.

This diversity added interest to our study. Some of the most interesting and valuable learning took place at the periodic conferences of associates where first-hand accounts were given of how the program was working in southern Florida, Houston, Chicago, Los Angeles, rural Mississippi, Maine, California, Oregon, South Dakota, and the variety of other places initially identified only by pins on a wall map.

Despite this variety, the similarities in responses to policy changes analyzed over four rounds of field observations were significant. Now that the PSE experiment is over, at least for the moment, we feel that these patterns allow us to draw some conclusions about the efficacy of public service employment under a variety of program designs and economic conditions. This chapter presents a brief summary of those conclusions, along with some observations about the future role of public service employment.

Our first observation is that even a very decentralized program operated by states and localities is quite responsive to major changes in direction at the federal level. As noted in chapter 1, the relative emphasis on various aspects of PSE varied considerably over time. Prior to 1976, the program was simply an optional CETA training program. Guidelines on the length of time that a person could participate in the program and limitations on wages that could be paid were liberal enough to allow good public service jobs with substantial tenure. The relatively lax standards on participant eligibility meant that state and local governments could use PSE to augment their regular workforce. Also, the potential for substitution of federal for state and local dollars was quite high.

Our study began in 1977 and coincided with a massive expansion of PSE for countercyclical purposes. While there is some question about the degree to which the program in this phase reached the economically disadvantaged, there is no doubt about the magnitude of the expansion or that state and local governments were able and willing to fill virtually all of the slots allotted to them by the federal government. Unlike traditional employment and training programs of the past, this buildup took place in an environment of excitement and energy. PSE was an opportunity for state and local governments to substantially increase government services without raising taxes, a feature that made it very attractive.

Because of the countercyclical emphasis of the program during this period, much attention was given to the question of displacement—the extent to which state and local governments used PSE in place of locally generated revenue. A crucial aspect of program effectiveness, this issue dominated the first two rounds of our study.

The key to this aspect of the field research was the development of a conceptual framework capable of capturing the ways in which job creation and displacement manifested themselves within the employment patterns of sponsoring agencies of government and nonprofit organizations. Within the established framework, the PSE employment process was analyzed in each of the sample jurisdictions, sometimes on a position-by-position basis. Estimates of displacement were particularly difficult to make where the essential question was whether an established position would have been abolished if it were not funded by PSE. This issue was most often faced in the larger cities of the Northeast and Midwest because so many of them were under extreme fiscal stress. It was the judgment of the field researchers in these areas that many positions funded by PSE in regular government activities were not displacement because those positions would have been eliminated had PSE funds not been available. The name we gave to this type of job creation was "program maintenance," and it proved a significant and inherently controversial component in measuring job creation.

Our findings indicated that the degree of displacement was much lower than others had predicted and, in fact, much lower than even some of us suspected prior to the study. On average, the displacement rate was about 20 percent, varying from almost zero to nearly 60 percent across jurisdictions. Rather than rising over time as some had predicted, the displacement rate was found to decline. We suspect that under a stable program, displacement rates would have increased as time passed. However, PSE was never stable and the trend toward a more tightly controlled program, particularly in participant eligibility requirements and allowable wage rates, did not allow that hypothesis to be tested. In effect, shifts over time dominated any movement toward a long term static equilibrium.

By the nature of the field research, we were also able to identify a benefit from PSE that was largely overlooked by national policymakers who focused primarily on the employment and training aspects of the program. That benefit was the value of the services provided by PSE and the importance of these services to local program operators. PSE workers did everything from providing library services to initiating "meals on wheels" programs for the aged. They were engaged in rat control programs in the cities, emergency medical services, park renovation, jogging trail construction, road repair, trail building, weed control, and record system modernization. The complete list for our sample jurisdictions is far too long to reproduce here.

It can be argued that these activities were marginal and of low value, a conclusion based on the notion that taxpayers did not care enough to pay for them with local tax money. That hypothesis is not directly testable, assumes stable priorities, and ignores demonstration effects. PSE allowed state and local officials the flexibility to direct marginal resources to the areas that they saw as most important. Many of these activities were continued after the PSE program ended.

Toward the end of the decade, when tighter restrictions on wages and participant eligibility limited the range of services that could be provided, we found that the program had lost much of its appeal to state and local officials. It is mainly because of this change that the Reagan administration's 1981 proposal to eliminate PSE was not more vigorously opposed. We suggest, therefore, that in future public policy deliberations over public service employment, explicit attention be paid to the types of services that PSE workers can provide; that some estimate of the value of these services be included in the benefit-cost calculation of such a program.

The training issue was the most difficult aspect of PSE to assess. In retrospect, it seems unfortunate that the informal training obtained by PSE participants in the regular performance of their public service jobs was largely overlooked as a positive aspect of the program. The difficulty in quantifying these training effects was undoubtedly one reason that greater emphasis was put on more formal and more costly classroom training during the last phase of the program. By contrast, only a very small percent of the money was allocated to formal training during the early countercyclical period of PSE, 1976-78. Yet the informal training aspects of PSE had an effect, as now confirmed by a study of the net earnings impact of the program, showing the earning gains by PSE participants equal to the average for all CETA programs.

It is our conclusion that PSE is an inappropriate program for those lacking basic skills, since the very concept of the program implies that a participant is capable of at least minimal job performance. However, on-the-job training provided in a regular job is useful for those with limited work experience, those who are re-entering the labor force, and those who have been displaced or dislocated by technological or economic change.

Another important program impact that is difficult to document and disentangle from other events during this time is the effect of PSE on the composition of the state and local government workforce. Because of the subsidies involved, PSE provided an incentive for governments to lower the education requirements for some positions, to employ women in traditionally male occupations, and to break down job entry barriers for minority groups. In several of our sample governments, we found that the wage subsidy was sufficient to cause even the most hardened personnel directors to consider changing some of their most discriminatory policies. There is also evidence that many "disadvantaged" PSE participants retained public sector jobs after they left the PSE program. We firmly believe that this experience helped remove some of the traditional obstacles to employment faced by those lacking educational credentials and by women and minorities and that this will be one of the most lasting impacts of the PSE program.

With all that's been learned, does PSE deserve a place among national policy options for increasing employment and providing equal opportunity? We firmly believe that it does. However, as suggested at the beginning of this book, PSE is not the elixir for all ailments, or even several at the same time. It does not seem to be appropriate for the most seriously disadvantaged, nor is it appropriate for those who are only temporarily inconvenienced by unemployment. It is, however, a program with great potential for those who are able to work and need job experience.

PSE should be administered subject to certain conditions. First, it should be prescribed for a limited period of time to avoid dependence by participants and excessive substitution by local governments and other employing agencies. Second, assuming that PSE participants are more disadvantaged than those who would normally receive on-the-job training in private sector positions, a case can be made for a higher subsidy rate and a longer tenure than the standard 50 percent wage subsidy, 6-month private sector OJT contract. The one-year limitation in the post-1978 PSE program seemed to have worked effectively in this regard.

Third, some limit should be placed on the maximum wage subsidy from federal funds both to control program costs and to assure that participants have an incentive to seek other employment. However, we do not support a limit on the ability of local governments to supplement the PSE maximum. We found no relation between local supplementation and displacement, and, in some cases, local areas were willing to create a job only if wages were sufficient to employ suitably qualified workers. Moreover, if combined with a limit on program tenure, such supplementation should not create a disincentive to find unsubsidized employment.

Fourth, because PSE is appropriately targeted on those who need work experience and on-the-job training but who are capable of holding a job at the outset of participation, we conclude that program eligibility criteria should be established in terms of labor market characteristics or labor market disadvantage rather than personal characteristics. Eligibility criteria should be defined by income level and employment experience rather than race, sex, age, or education. Education, however, is sufficiently correlated with labor market disadvantage that those without a high school degree will represent a significant segment of the eligible population.

Finally, effective implementation of a locally administered program like PSE requires sensitivity to the objectives of local program operators. Without recognizing this vital aspect of program design, it is unlikely that any future PSE initiative will succeed. The experience of the 1970s provides clear instruction about incentives associated with public service employment and essential design criteria to reach program goals. In this nation of diversity there is at least one constant across all areas; namely, everyone is looking for a bargain. Our research indicates that, if properly designed, PSE can provide employment and training for participants, some easing of the twin demands for tax relief and additional services from state and local governments, and progress toward the federal goals of expanded employment, equal opportunity, and a better-trained workforce. That's a pretty good bargain, with one important caveat. As any one party to the bargain tries to get too much, it is likely to undermine the entire process.

While any new public employment program must be carefully designed and planned, the concept itself remains viable. For as long as there is concern about unemployment and untrained workers, there is a policy role for public service employment.